The Culture of Surveillance
Discipline and Social Control
in the United States

Contemporary Social Issues

George Ritzer, Series Editor

Urban Enclaves: Identity and Place in America
Mark Abrahamson, *University of Connecticut*

The Wilding of America: How Greed and Violence Are Eroding Our Nation's Character
Charles Derber, *Boston College*

Between Politics and Reason: The Drug Legalization Debate
Erich Goode, *State University of New York, Stony Brook*

The Culture of Surveillance: Discipline and Social Control in the United States
William G. Staples, *University of Kansas*

Forthcoming

The Myth of Self-Esteem
John P. Hewitt, *University of Massachusetts, Amherst*

Contemporary Social Issues

Series Editor: George Ritzer, University of Maryland

The Culture of Surveillance
Discipline and Social Control
in the United States

William G. Staples

University of Kansas

St. Martin's Press
New York

To William C. and Anna M. Staples, with love

Editor-in-chief: Steve Debow
Manager, publishing services: Emily Berleth
Senior editor, publishing services: Doug Bell
Production supervisor: Joe Ford
Project management: Richard Steins
Composition: Ewing Systems
Cover design: Patricia McFadden
Cover photo: Copyright © Jill Enfield

Library of Congress Catalog Card Number: 95-73185

Manufactured in the United States of America.
1 0 9 8 7
f   e   d c b a

For information, write:
St. Martin's Press, Inc.
175 Fifth Avenue
New York NY 10010

ISBN: 0-312-11962-3 (softcover)
ISBN: 0-312-17280-X (hardcover)

Contents

Foreword

As we move toward the close of the twentieth century, we confront a seemingly endless array of pressing social issues: crime, urban decay, inequality, ecological threats, rampant consumerism, war, AIDS, inadequate health care, national and personal debt, and many more. Although such problems are regularly dealt with in newspapers, magazines, and trade books and on radio and television, such popular treatment has severe limitations. By examining these issues systematically through the lens of sociology, we can gain greater insight into them and be better able to deal with them. It is to this end that St. Martin's Press has created this series on contemporary social issues.

Each book in the series casts a new and distinctive light on a familiar social issue, while challenging the conventional view, which may obscure as much as it clarifies. Phenomena that seem disparate and unrelated are shown to have many commonalities and to reflect a major, but largely unrecognized, trend within the larger society. Or a systematic comparative investigation demonstrates the existence of social causes or consequences that are overlooked by other types of analysis. In uncovering such realities the books in this series are much more than intellectual exercises; they have powerful practical implications for our lives and for the structure of society.

At another level, this series fills a void in book publishing. There is certainly no shortage of academic titles, but those books tend to be introductory texts for undergraduates or advanced monographs for professional scholars. Missing are broadly accessible, issue-oriented books appropriate for all students (and for general readers). The books in this series occupy that niche somewhere between popular trade books and monographs. Like trade books, they deal with important and interesting social issues, are well written, and are as jargon free as possible. However, they are more rigorous than trade books in meeting academic standards for writing and research. Although they are not textbooks, they often explore topics covered in basic textbooks and therefore are easily integrated into the curriculum of sociology and other disciplines.

Each of the books in the St. Martin's series "Contemporary Social Issues" is a new and distinctive piece of work. I believe that students, serious general readers, and professors will all find the books to be informative, interesting, thought provoking, and exciting.

George Ritzer

Preface

Entering a large discount store recently, I was struck at the contrast between the welcoming, human smile of the "greeter" positioned in the lobby and, right behind her, the unblinking stare of the videocam that was projecting my image on a nearby screen. As I stood taking in the scene, some little kids joined in, jumping up and down, watching themselves on the monitor. Mom spoiled the fun, however, protectively hustling them out of the range of the camera. Yet even she could not resist glancing back over her shoulder as her own image flashed across the screen.

As sociologist Wendy Griswold points out, we study "culture" when we observe a community's pattern of meanings; its enduring expressive aspects; its symbols that represent and guide the thinking, feelings, and behavior of its members. The word surveillance, in the most general sense, refers to the act of keeping a close watch on people. The purpose of this book is to examine the meanings, attitudes, and behaviors surrounding the ways in which people in the United States are increasingly being watched, monitored, and controlled in their everyday lives. I characterize this aspect of contemporary life then as "the culture of surveillance."

Rejecting the of the idea of a highly coordinated, state-driven, "Big Brother" monopoly over the practice of watching people, I focus on the "micro" techniques of discipline that target and treat the body as an object to be watched, assessed, and manipulated. These are "local" knowledge-gathering activities—often enhanced by the use of new information, visual, communication, and medical technologies—that are increasingly present in the workplace, the school, the home, and the community. In this book I argue that while our inherited, "modern" ideas about the nature of human beings, deviance, and social control continue to shape the ways in which we "keep a close watch on people," a new set of meanings, attitudes, and practices is taking hold that is constituted by and indicative of conditions of postmodernity.

This book was written to be accessible to a wide audience. While deeply informed by the work of social historians and theorists, my approach is relatively free of academic jargon. It is particularly suited as a supplemental text for students taking classes such as Introduction to Sociology, Social Problems, Deviance and Social Control, Crime and Society, American Society, and the like. Many of the positions I take will be considered provocative at the very least. My intent is to challenge the reader to come face to face with what I believe to be one of the most significant issues of our day and to consider it from what is likely to be an alternative vantage point. My hope is that you will find the book enjoyable, informative, and worthy of considerable discussion and debate.

ACKNOWLEDGMENTS

This project was supported, in part, by the sabbatical leave program and a grant from the General Research Fund of the University of Kansas. I appreciate very much the work of my undergraduate research assistants Sarah Flood, Sharareh Hersemy, and Angela Marks. I would also like to recognize the people who were willing to share with me their work, lives, and experiences that have become part of this book. While their identities remain hidden, their impact has been profound. Thanks go to the students from my seminar in the History of Social Control, especially David Barney, Ben Coates, Kevin Gotham, Jennifer Hackney, and Dan Krier.

The editorial staff at St. Martin's Press and I appreciate the valuable comments and suggestions of the following people who kindly reviewed this manuscript: Patricia Clough, CUNY—Graduate School and University Center; Mark Gottdiener, University of California, Riverside; Travis Hirschi, University of Arizona; John Kramer, Penn State University; Gary Marx, University of Colorado, Boulder; and Austin Turk, University of California, Riverside.

I am also grateful for the comments and suggestions I received from David Altheide, Bob Antonio, Norman Denzin, Sue Lorenz, Joane Nagel, Mike Schwalbe, David Smith, Cliff Staples, and Carol Warren. Thanks also to Ed Stanford at St. Martin's Press for his faith in the project, Steve Debow for shepherding it through the final stages, and Hanna Shinn, editorial assistant extraordinaire, for being there when I needed her. Finally, it was George Ritzer who first approached me about doing this book and who provided invaluable feedback as consulting editor. I thank him very much for the opportunity and his advice.

About the Author

William G. Staples grew up on the south shore of Long Island, New York. He has been a commercial fisherman, taxicab driver, plumber's apprentice, and pizza chef. He studied sociology at the University of Oregon, went on to receive his Ph.D. from the University of Southern California, and spent two years as postdoctoral fellow at the University of California, Los Angeles. Staples is currently associate professor of sociology and director of graduate studies at the University of Kansas. He is the author of *Castles of Our Conscience: Social Control and the American State, 1800–1985* (1991) and is coeditor of the journal *Sociological Inquiry.* He lives in Lawrence, Kansas, with his son, Ian.

1

The Culture of Surveillance

Today, nearly ninety percent of U.S. manufacturers are testing workers for drug use. . . . In California and Texas, every citizen wishing to be issued a driver's license must have their thumb print computer scanned. . . . In Kansas, school children are identified with "bar codes" so that a teacher can use a computer to track their daily behavioral and academic performance. . . . In Maine, a police officer whose name is simply raised in a local sex-abuse case is told he has to submit to a test designed to measure his "sexual desire." . . . In Arizona, a "welfare mother" has a court-ordered contraceptive device surgically implanted in her arm. . . . And, in nearly every state in the country, convicted felons are placed under "house arrest," their movements monitored electronically by a transmitter attached to their ankle.

The preceding examples were headline news in the last couple of years. How are we to understand these developments? Are they simply "advances" in our struggle against illegal or "deviant" behavior, or do they signal the rise of what might be called a "culture of surveillance"? What kind of society has produced these practices, and why do we appear so willing to adopt them? The purpose of this book is to explore these and other questions about the emergence of new forms of social control in contemporary society.

Recently, I sat in the "cafe" section of a large, suburban bookstore talking with a friend. She asked me what I was working on these days, and I told her that I was writing a book about discipline and social control in contemporary life. At this she said, "You mean about all the crime and prisons?" "No," I said, "not really. More like the issue of surveillance." "Oh," she replied, "so you are looking into how the FBI spies on people?"

To many of us, including my friend, issues of discipline, social control, and surveillance tend either to revolve around the criminal justice system or to invite the image of George Orwell's notorious "Big Brother." Yet as important as the prison system and the activities of domestic "spying" organizations are, I am more interested here in the relatively small, often mundane procedures and practices—the "Tiny Brothers" if you will—that are increasingly present in our daily lives. These techniques exist in the shadow of large institutions like prisons; they are not ushered in with dramatic displays of state power like the Branch Davidian stand-off in Waco, Texas, nor do they appear as significant challenges to constitutional democracy such as the FBI's COunterINTELligence programs of the 1960s and 1970s. The techniques I mean are the more common-place strategies used by both governmental and private organizations to "keep us in line," monitor our performance, gather evidence, assess deviations, and, if necessary, exact penalties. For it is these daily activities that involve many more, if not all, of us than does life in a state prison or the latest FBI "sting" operation.

The techniques I have in mind range along a continuum. They begin with the "soft," seemingly benign and relatively inconspicuous forms of monitoring and control such as the those used by the very bookstore where I sat with my friend. In that business, as in thousands across the United States, a security system monitored our interaction with video cameras, while the store's spatial arrangement was designed for optimal surveillance of customers and employees alike. Computerized checkout stations keep track of inventory, calculate store performance figures, assess the credit worthiness of customers through remote databanks, and monitor the "logon" and "logoff" times of employees. They can even cal-culate the average number of customers those employees processed per hour. And, of course, the store had "tagged" all the merchandise so that each of us could be electronically "frisked" as we left. All this was accom-plished behind the scene, without disruption to the manufactured ambiance of soft leather chairs, melodic Muzak, and the sound and smell of cappuccino-making.

At the "hard" end of the spectrum are the more obtrusive and more confrontational practices that often begin with the assumption of guilt and are designed to uncover the "truth," to test an individual's character, and, more generally, to make people consciously aware that they are indeed being watched and monitored. These are what I call "surveillance ceremonies" such as random drug testing, the use of lie detectors, pre-employment integrity tests, and sobriety "checkpoints" in the streets.

Between these soft and hard types of social control lies a vast array of techniques and technologies—exercised on people both inside and outside the "official" legal system—designed to watch our bodies, to reg-ulate our activities and movements, and, ultimately, to shape or change our behavior. These procedures are often taken in the name of law and order, public safety, the protection of private property, or sound business practice; other procedures are initiated for an individual's "own good" or benefit. But no matter what the stated motivation, the intent is to shape and modify actions and behaviors.

The subject of this book then are the cultural practices that I will call "meticulous rituals of power." Most generally, I include those "micro" techniques of discipline and social control that are often enhanced by the use of new information, communications, and medical technologies. These are knowledge-gathering activities that involve surveillance, information, and evidence collection and analysis. I call them *meticulous* because they are "small" procedures and techniques that are precisely and thoroughly exercised. I see them as *ritualistic* because they are faithfully repeated and are often quickly accepted and routinely practiced with little question. And they are about *power* because they are intended to discipline people into acting in ways that others have deemed to be lawful or have defined as appropriate or simply "normal." In this way, *meticulous rituals* are the specific, concrete mechanisms that operate to maintain unbalanced and unequal authority relationships. These relationships exist between specific clusters of individuals (e.g., between managers and workers, police officers and suspects, probation officials and offenders, teachers and students, parents and children, etc.) and, in a larger sense, between individuals and the public and private organizations where these rituals take place.[1]

"OK," you may say, "so what is really new here?" Hasn't society always had ways of "keeping people in line?" Aren't these "meticulous rituals" just newer, perhaps more effective ways of doing what we have always done to ensure social order? In some ways, yes, they are indeed logical extensions of "modern" solutions to the problems of crime, deviance, and social control, and they may indeed be more efficient. Yet, at the same time, they have qualities that make them fundamentally new, and, I want to argue, more *post*modern in design and implementation, and I think it's important that we come to understand the implications of their use. I see at least four defining characteristics that set these practices apart from more "traditional" methods.

In the first place, consider the following. In the past, the watchful eyes of a small shopkeeper may have deterred a would-be shoplifter, her surveillance was personal, not terribly systematic, and her memory, of course, was fallible. She was more likely to know her customers (and they her), to keep a "closer eye" on strangers, and to "look the other way" when she saw fit (and to make a call to the offending juveniles' parents later). This kind of "personal" social control was once typical of small communities or close-knit societies where people certainly watch one another very closely and where fear of ridicule or exclusion is a powerful inducement to conformity. By contrast, the part-time, nonowning employees of the large corporate bookstore where I sat with my friend

have less interest in watching for thieves; their huge number of customers are an anonymous crowd. So here, the store management relies
on the hidden, faceless, and ever-ready video security camera. The videocam—one of the defining traits of postmodern society—projects a
*hyper*vigilant "gaze" randomly scanning the entire store day or night,
recording every event, and watching *all* the customers, not just the "suspicious ones." The cameras are also positioned to watch the vast number
of employees as well, who must now be monitored both as "productive"
workers and as potential thieves. In this way, surveillance and discipline
have become oddly democratic; everyone is watched, and *no one* is trusted. So the first characteristic of postmodern social control is that it tends
to be systematic, methodical, and automatic in operation. It is more likely "impersonal" in that the "observer" is rarely seen and is anonymous;
even more likely, "they" are a computer system, a videocam, a drug-test-
ing kit, or an electronic scanner of some kind. Once more, the data that
these devices collect may become part of a permanent record in the form
of a videotape, computer file, and the like. In fact, persons being monitored are often unaware that the knowledge about them even exists.

Second, these new meticulous rituals of power often involve our
bodies in new and important ways, and I want to distinguish two primary tactics of bodily social control. I agree with Donald Lowe when he
states: "As living beings, we are more than body and mind, more than the
representations and images of our body. We lead a bodily life in the
world."[2] These bodily lives are shaped, manipulated, and controlled by a
set of ongoing practices that compose our daily lives as workers, consumers, and community members. The first tactic I want to distinguish
has to do with types of monitoring and surveillance that enhance our
visibility to others. We seem to be entering a state of "permanent visibility" where attempts to control and shape our behavior—in essence, our
bodies—is accomplished not so much by the threat of punishment and
physical force but by the act of being watched—continuously, anonymously, and automatically. This kind of watching happens when people
engage in such diverse activities as clipping on a company beeper, using
a credit card to purchase something at a store, or parking their car in a
garage with a security camera. These instances signify different forms of
"visibility": the beeper enables an employer to remotely "check up" on
and monitor an employee; the credit card purchase leaves an electronic
paper trail of a person's whereabouts; and the security camera identifies
to the police, or anyone else, that a particular individual indeed parked
in that garage on a particular day at a certain time. The methodical, technology-driven, impersonal gaze, I argue, is quickly becoming a primary
mechanism of social control in our society, and it is fixed on our bodies
and their movements.

A second tactic of bodily social control relates to new developments in science, technology, and medical knowledge. These intersecting fields are making the human body infinitely more accessible to official scrutiny and assessment. This means that the ability of organizations to monitor, judge, or even regulate our actions and behaviors *through our bodies* is significantly enhanced. It also means that it becomes less important to trust suspects to "speak the truth" or convicted offenders to "mend their ways." Rather, it is the individual's body that will "tell us what we need to know," as in indicating that someone is using drugs or was at the scene of a crime or even has "deviant desires." In this way, the body is treated as an "object" that contains the evidence of any possible deviance. For example, on the soft side of our spectrum of social control, we see that corporations are using medical data collected on employees in their "wellness" and exercise clinics to confront the "unhealthy lifestyles" of those not conforming to prevailing standards (about, e.g., tobacco use or obesity). Meanwhile, on the hard side, DNA samples are being systematically collected and stored and are increasingly presented as evidence in courtroom proceedings. The body, I contend, is a central target of many postmodern disciplinary techniques and rituals.

The third defining characteristic relates to a shift in the location of formal social control and which behaviors are the subject of it. Since the early nineteenth century, our primary method of dealing with lawbreakers, those thought to be insane, other deviants, and even the poor has been to isolate them *from* everyday life—as in the case of the modern prison, mental asylum, and reformatory. Yet the kinds of practices I am most concerned with here attempt to impose a framework of accountability on an individual *in* everyday life. While, obviously, removing "troublesome" people from society is still a significant means of formal social control (after all, in the United States, we institutionalize more people than any other Western country does), this approach is increasingly considered an inefficient, ineffective, and undesirable practice. This is particularly true if we consider the idea that as a society we seem to be engaged in a far-reaching attempt to regulate not only the traditional crimes of person and property but also the behaviors, conditions, and lifestyles of substance (ab)use, alcohol and tobacco consumption, "eating disorders," forms of sexual expression and sexual "promiscuity" and "deviance," teenage pregnancy, out-of-marriage births, domestic violence, child abuse, "dysfunctional" families, various psychological or psychiatric disorders and other medical conditions such as "attention deficit disorder," and such diseases as AIDS. How can we possibly institutionalize and control everyone who falls into these rapidly expanding categories of "troublesome" individuals?

Under these conditions, it would appear that the segregative or "quarantine" models of social control of the nineteenth century are an invention whose time has simply passed. The incentive now is to develop new ways to control and "keep an eye on" what appears to be an increasing number of "deviants" through an expanding network of formal "community corrections" programs; regulatory welfare, health, and social service agencies; and even schools, workplaces, and other community institutions. New developments in the forensic, medical, and computer and information sciences—generated by corporate research and development departments and the post–Cold War military-industrial complex (which I believe is being converted rapidly into a "security-industrial complex")—are creating more remote, more flexible, and more efficient ways of making this happen.

Finally, as new forms of social control are "localized" in everyday life, they are capable of bringing wide-ranging populations, not just the "official" deviant, under their watchful gaze. As I indicated earlier, trust is becoming a rare commodity in our culture. The notion of "innocent until proven guilty" seems like so much the cliché these days when people are apt to be subjected to a disciplinary ritual and surveillance ceremonies simply because "statistics" indicate that they have the potential for being offenders. Data generated through surveillance techniques produce "types" or whole classes of individuals who are deemed "at risk" for behavior, whether any one particular individual has engaged in such behavior or not. These data, of course, are then used to justify even closer surveillance and scrutiny of this group, thereby increasing the likelihood of uncovering more offenses; and so it goes. In this context, social control becomes more about predicting and preventing deviance—always assuming that it *will* indeed happen—rather than responding to a violation after it has occurred. Therefore, when put in place, ritualistic monitoring and surveillance ceremonies often blur the distinction between the "official" deviant and the "likely" or even "possible" offender. Indeed, what separates the convicted felon, the college athlete, or the discount store cashier if all are subjected to random drug screening? One consequence of this blurring is that we may be witnessing a historical shift from the specific punishment of the individual deviant to the generalized surveillance of us all.

But by implying that social control is becoming more universal and thus oddly more democratic, I am *not* suggesting that we are all necessarily subject to the same quantity or quality of social control. Historically and cross-culturally, the amount and character of discipline and punishment that individuals are afforded have varied considerably by such defining characteristics as race, ethnicity, class, and gender. This continues today without question. My point is that today there are *more* impersonal, more methodical, and more technology-driven forms of surveillance and social control in our society than ever before, and that today's forms—and their shear volume—are enveloping even those who might have been previously exempt. For those who have traditionally been the target of monitoring and control, these developments serve only to intensify and increase the amount of formal regulation already in their daily lives.

So it would seem that while these meticulous rituals are "more of the same," they are, in other respects, strikingly new; and this, I propose, is how we should come to understand them. In other words, we need to see how the world we are creating today is a product of both our *modern* historical past and our *postmodern* cultural present. This historically grounded perspective has two advantages. First, if we connect these "new" disciplinary techniques to significant long-term processes and trends, we can see the *continuity* of social life and can understand that contemporary developments reflect an ongoing struggle to deal with problems and issues set in motion with the birth of the modern age. Second, by looking at how differently we have responded to the problems of social order in the past, we can also see that matters of deviance and social control are not fixed categories but are *changing, socially constructed* ideas. Therefore we begin to realize that what is defined as "deviant" or as "social problems" today—as well as what seem like appropriate responses to them—may not have been considered worthy of attention one hundred years ago or even ten years ago.

These long-term changes I refer to are some of the major themes that have come to characterize the period of modernity (from around 1790 until the 1950s) and have had considerable influence on our strategies of social control. These themes include the increasing rationalization of social life; the rise of large, centralized states and private organizations; and strongly held beliefs in reason and rationality as well as in the certainty of "progress." This modern faith in our power to shape the world was grounded in our apparent ability to control and to "know" nature through the physical sciences. This model of science was increasing applied to the manipulation of "man" through the knowledge of the "human sciences" such as medicine, criminology, psychology, sociology, demography, and the like. In other words, with the birth of the modern era, human beings—our bodies, minds, and behaviors—became the *subject* or topic of scientific inquiry as well as the *object* or target of its knowledge. Thus, we see in the modern era the gradual disappearance of public torture and stigmatization as the primary means of punishment and social control, and their replacement by rationally organized reformatory institutions such as the prison, the poorhouse, and the asylum. Rather than seek retribution and public punishment, these institutions would isolate the offending individual and introduce behavioral modification—the transformation of the criminal, the deviant, and the poor—

through the administration of techniques of knowledge and power. Many of these influences are still with us today and continue to shape social life. It is this relationship—between knowledge and power—that is central to the operation of meticulous rituals.

At the same time, however, there is evidence that a new social order is emerging out this older, modern one. This *post*modern society, originating in developments since World War II, and more intensely since the early 1970s, is a culture deeply penetrated by commodities and consumer "lifestyles." In our day it would seem that consumption rather than production has become the wellspring of society, while highly bureaucratic (although increasingly "decentralized") state agencies attempt to order and regulate social life. Ours is a culture characterized by fragmentation and uncertainty as many of the once-taken-for-granted meanings, symbols, and institutions of modern life dissolve before our eyes. Time as well as social and geographical space are highly compressed by rapidly changing computer and advanced technologies, information storage and retrieval, and scientific/medical knowledge.

What is "real" in this culture is presented to us through the mass media in video imagery that has become the primary source of our cultural knowledge. We are offered a nonstop barrage of "crisis-level" social problems, leaving us wondering "what the world is coming to." In turn, we are left cynically mistrusting each other—and furthering the disintegration of public life and discourse. This cultural hysteria creates a fertile ground for those selling "science" and the seemingly innocent technological fixes that they claim will ease our fears. Under these conditions, we turn to more pervasive, rational, and predictable means of surveillance and social control. In essence, we are seduced into believing that subjecting ourselves to more and more "meticulous rituals" is an unfortunate but necessary condition given the apparent tide of problems we face. The forgoing conditions form what I will refer to simply as "the everyday life of the postmodern," and it is in this cultural context, I believe, that we continue to struggle with problems and issues which arose during the early nineteenth century.

As an example how our current disciplinary practices are a product of both our historical past and our cultural present, let us consider an incident that took place recently in my hometown. In this case, a school bus driver was accused of physically restraining an unruly child. The driver was fired, and much debate took place in the local newspaper about the children's behavior on the bus, the reported good reputation of the driver, and about the way school district administrators (mis)handled the case. It was clear that no one seemed to trust anyone's account of what had actually transpired on the bus that day. A few months later there was an announcement that each of the district's fleet of new buses would be equipped with a video camera "black box." The company claimed that, on any given day, just three video cameras would be rotated among all the district's buses and that, given the design of the boxes, neither the students nor the drivers would know when their bus was equipped with a camera. The bus company's manager stated that the images and sounds captured by the camera "helps improve student discipline" as well as ensures that the drivers are following "proper procedures."

Now, the principle behind the rotating camera is not new; it originates with a design dating from 1791 for a central guard tower inside a prison or reformatory. The tower was constructed in such a way that prisoners were never quite sure whether a guard was present or not and would have to assume that they were being watched. The inmates, then, in effect, watched themselves, "internalizing" if you will, the gaze of the keeper. It was a simple, even elegant, solution to the problem of disciplining people in an enclosed space—a dilemma brought about with the birth of the asylum, the modern "solution" to criminal behavior, madness, poverty, and the like. The evolution of this idea two hundred years later—and applied in a postmodern context—produces a flexible design, routinely applied in the everyday life of schoolchildren and their adult supervisors, none of whom apparently are trusted to act responsibly. Inexpensive video technology—and our willingness to define schoolchildren's behavior on a bus as being so problematic that it warrants "objective" surveillance rather than personal monitoring—makes the use of this new form of social control possible. Curious about what people thought of the cameras, I spoke with friends and others in the community about the new policy. Most seemed shocked at the idea at first, but then, in resignation, many would concede that it was probably a "good idea" for the "safety" of everyone involved. I see the new disciplinary techniques then, *both* as a product of important, long-term processes set in motion more than two centuries ago and as being shaped by a newly emerging cultural context.

I am *not* suggesting that there is no need for social control in our society or that shoplifting, drug abuse, and violent crime are not *real* problems with *real* victims. Of course they are. Having lived in Los Angeles for nearly a decade, I have witnessed firsthand the crime, violence, and chronic social problems that seems to define the hard edge of U.S. urban life. But the issues I am raising are of broader, sociological concern and have to do with the "big picture" of where we are going as a culture and with the balance of power, if you will, in that larger society. In other words, I want to look at the evolution of discipline and punishment as not simply a judicial matter but as an entry point to understanding our changing attitude toward social control in general. I want to first dispel any notion that the last two hundred or so years of "reforming" justice practice has unequivocally produced a system that is more "just" or more "humane" than the brutal, public punishment that came before it. Therefore, I want to challenge the idea that, simply put, we keep building a better mousetrap. Rather, I want to argue that the modern attempt to transform, mold, shape, and "rehabilitate" the criminal, the deviant, and the poor in the name of more effective and even progressive social policy may, in fact, be seen as a more general model for the rational ordering of the entire society. That is, I am concerned here with a process, set in motion in the early nineteenth century, whereby the enforcement of ever-finer distinctions between what is "acceptable" and "unacceptable" behavior has become part of all our daily lives, and not just the lives of those who break the law. Ultimately, I will show how we are indeed building a "culture of surveillance" when we infuse daily life with practices that constantly assess our behavior, judge our performance, account for our whereabouts, and challenge our personal integrity by assuming that we are guilty until proven innocent.

Let us consider another contemporary example. I find it remarkable how quickly people will agree to give up their constitutional right to freedom of movement in order to stop what some claim to be rampant drunk-driving behavior. We accept this, despite the evidence that so-called sobriety checkpoints apprehend very few excessive drinkers. Supporters of these bodily-based "surveillance ceremonies" contend that "if you have nothing to hide, you have nothing to fear"; yet we know from experience that unbridled police powers are likely to present a serious challenge to individual liberties. Obviously, even one person injured or killed by a drunk driver is a tragedy, but it might be argued that creating a police state to thwart the behavior may be an even greater catastrophe. As Supreme Court Justice John Paul Stevens declared in his dissenting opinion on the legality of such roadblocks, "Unfortunately the Court is transfixed by the wrong symbol—the illusory prospect of punishing countless intoxicated motorists—when it should keep its eyes on the road plainly marked by the Constitution."[3] Why not focus our efforts on education and safety programs (funded by the businesses that sell and benefit from the sale of alcohol)?

Next, consider the proliferation of metal detectors and bodily searchers, not simply at airports but also in schools, courthouses, dance clubs, and the like, to thwart the possession of weapons. (Ironically, at the same time, several states are passing or are considering laws that *permit* people to carry concealed weapons.) Rather than seriously confront the issue of the widespread availability of guns in our society (in this case, a "right" clearly *not* protected under the Constitution's Second Amendment clause concerning a "well regulated Militia" and not permitted in any other "developed" country), we subject all citizens to this kind of daily surveillance and monitoring. This, it seems, may be the most fundamental question raised by this book: Are we, in our attempts to preserve our freedom and security, entrapping ourselves in our own solutions?

Before we can debate such questions, however, I need to explain more fully the origins of my perspective on the changing nature of discipline and social control. I begin Chapter 2 by focusing on the work of the late French philosopher Michel Foucault (1926–1984). It is from Foucault, a pioneering social theorist, that I take the idea to concentrate on the small, seemingly benign rituals at the intersection of power, knowledge, and the body. In his strikingly original book *Discipline and Punish*, Foucault presented a political history of two basic forms of discipline: the physical torture associated with the "Age of the Sovereign" and, later, the emergence of the asylum, a product of modernity.[4] Building on Foucault's analysis, in this book I will chart the evolution of disciplinary practices from the invention of the asylum on, and, by taking up where Foucault left off, I hope to extend his study of modern social control into the *post*modern era.

As I have noted in this chapter, contemporary disciplinary practices have four characteristics:

1. They are increasingly technology-based, methodical, automatic, and sometimes anonymously applied, and they usually generate a permanent record as evidence.

2. Many new techniques target and treat the body as an object that can be watched, assessed, and manipulated.

3. The new techniques are often "local," operating in our everyday lives.

4. Local or not, they manage to bring wide-ranging populations, not just the "official" deviant, under scrutiny.

These characteristics form a "descriptive type" for what I am calling "meticulous rituals of power." The central purpose of Chapters 3 and 4 is to use this classification scheme to identify and examine these cultural practices and the locations where they take place. In these chapters I will be drawing on examples from and moving back and fourth between the official justice system and our everyday postmodern life. In Chapter 3, I will focus on new forms of surveillance that systematically watch and monitor our bodies and behaviors; I will show how our communities, homes, schools, and workplaces are increasing infused with meticulous rituals and surveillance ceremonies. In Chapter 4, I turn my attention to practices that treat the body itself as the site and source of evidence and knowledge or, alternatively, that attempt to take control of the body through the use of various technologies. Finally, in Chapter 5, I will return to considering the important questions I have raised in this introduction about these contemporary developments, assess their consequences, and consider what the future may hold.

NOTES

1. These ideas were pursued in some of my earlier work. See "Small Acts of Cunning: Disciplinary Practices in Contemporary Life." *Sociological Quarterly* 35, 1994: 645–64; and Dan Krier and William G. Staples, "Seen But Unseen: Part-time Faculty and Institutional Surveillance and Control." *American Sociologist* 24, 1994: 119–34.
2. Donald Lowe, *The Body in Late Capitalism USA*. Durham, N.C.: Duke University Press, 1995.
3. "Excerpts from Supreme Court Decision." *New York Times*, June 15, 1990: A11.
4. Michel Foucault, *Discipline and Punish: The Birth of the Prison*. Trans. A. M. Sheridan. New York: Pantheon, 1977.

2

The Scaffold,
the Penitentiary, and Beyond

In the colony of Virginia during the 1760s, the theft of a hog would bring

> *twenty-five lashes well laid on at the publick whipping post;*
> *for the second offense he was set two houres in the pillory and*
> *had both ears nailed ther to, at the end of the two hours to have*
> *the ears slit loose; for the third offence, death. . . .*[1]

Yet by the 1830s,

> *Within an atmosphere of repression, humiliation, and gloomy*
> *silence, the Auburn Penitentiary convict performed an incessantly*
> *monotonous round of activity. He arose at 5:15 and as soon as his*
> *cell was unlocked, he marched out holding three pieces of equipment:*
> *a night tub used for calls of nature; a can for drinking water; and*
> *a wooden food container. Holding this paraphilia in his left hand, he*
> *laid his right hand on the shoulder of the felon who occupied the next*
> *cell and marched in lock-step across the court yard to his workshop.*[2]

Here we have two *very* different forms of punishment. What happened to bring about this radical change in social control? For years, legal scholars and historians advanced the idea that the "invention" of the modern penitentiary was a product of a deep, humanitarian impulse on the part of reformers, the public, and state officials. From this perspective, the ritualized torture on the public scaffold used in Europe and the whipping post favored in the United States were, quite suddenly, deemed barbaric and unenlightened, and, if one reads the rhetoric of the reformers of the nineteenth century, this theme is certainly evident. Yet, in recent years, some people have come to question this interpretation. One significant figure in that debate is Michel Foucault.

Foucault argued that while indeed the penal reformers of the eighteenth century may have set out to reduce the ferocity of punishment—
along with its public spectacle—they did not necessarily aim to punish
less but, rather, to punish *better*. In other words, their intent was to make
punishment and the system of justice more efficient and effective.
Punishment, under their plan, would be rationally organized and pro-
portional to the crime; deterrence, rather than retribution, would be its
central purpose. These ideas helped set in motion a series of "reforms" by
which, among other things, the "soul" as well as the body of the offender became the target of punishment. The perpetrator would now be sent
away for years to the modern asylum, such as the Auburn penitentiary,
and was subjected to an institutional regime that would isolate his mind
and discipline his body. The staff would watch his every move, accumu-
late knowledge of the circumstances of his crime, his family background,
and life history. It would break him of his bad habits and transform him
into a model citizen. Punishment would succeed when the inmate had
been "rehabilitated."

But Foucault, in a book entitled *Surveiller et punir: Naissance de la
prison* and translated from the French to *Discipline and Punish: The Birth
of the Prison,* questions the very notion that all this has *necessarily* meant
"progress" and the more "humane" treatment of the offender.[3] Indeed,
we might want to ask ourselves: Is more or less physical pain the only
yardstick of benevolence? Of suffering? Of human dignity? On what
basis and with what values do we assess whether a deviant is treated more
"humanly"? On what scale, for example, do we place ten lashes versus ten
years in prison for a "three strikes and you're out" offense? I am not advocating a return to physical punishment but rather questioning the philosophical and ethical basis on which claims of "justice" and "humanity"
have been asserted. Such claims can often appear quite contradictory.
Take the case of the young American in Singapore in 1994 who was sentenced to six lashes from a rattan cane for vandalism. Following the sentence there were cries of brutality and "inhumane" treatment from U.S.
officials. Curiously, at nearly that same time, a criminologist and longtime death penalty proponent in New York was calling for the substitution of lethal injection for the electric chair to carry out that state's recent
return to executions. He claimed that the injections were a "painless and
nonrepulsive way of doing justice."[4] This suggests that, for some, even a
death sentence can be considered "humane" as long as it is "painless."

With the purported "march of progress," then, while it may be said
that social control has, in some ways, become more "lenient," even "gen-
tle," it may also be true that it has become more widespread and more
invasive. What do I mean? Simply this: That changes begun in the early
nineteenth century to make justice more "efficient" set in motion a

process whereby the authority to judge an individual's behavior has been extended well beyond the legal offense committed. Since that time, a complex machinery of organizations, institutions, and practices (e.g., different kinds of jails, prisons, courts, probation and parole systems, halfway houses, community corrections programs, and the like) has been developing and is now part of the justice system. The result has been a proliferation of the number of "crimes" it is possible to commit as well as the number of "judges" to assess them. These judges are the armies of personnel who appear as "expert" authorities such as probation officers, wardens, psychiatrists, social workers, criminologists, penologists, and the like, along with their diagnoses, assessments, evaluations, and classifications. In fact, rather than simply responding to a specific behavior or infraction, this kind of judgment goes beyond simply what someone has *done* and extends to the very core of *who they are.* In other words, this "power to punish" assesses something other than crimes alone. It judges what kind of persons offenders are and whether they measure up to the kind of person society wants them to be. This book is not only about how this power to punish, and the making of ever-finer distinctions between what is "acceptable" and "unacceptable" behavior, has taken hold in the official justice system but also about how it has spread to communities, workplaces, schools, homes, and most spheres of social life. It is about, in essence, the enforcement of "normalcy" and the attempt to eliminate all social, physical, and psychological "irregularities."

Seen in this way, a man who stole a hog in the colony of Virginia was simply *punished* for his crime. No one expected him, as part of his penalty, to reflect on his inner self or to become a productive worker. No one really cared if he came from a "dysfunctional" family, if he had a "personality disorder," or if he was a good candidate for "rehabilitation." While there is little doubt that torturing the hog thief was a brutish act, there were limits to how much pain and punishment could be exacted on him without killing him (which, of course, effectively ended his punishment). His body was all he had to offer; it was all that the authorities could take from him. Yet, at some point, it was decided that, no, the thief had more to give; it not was enough that he simply stop stealing hogs. Reformers, philosophers, jurists, and state officials began to argue that, with the right program, the criminal, the deviant, the delinquent, and even the poor could be "morally reformed"—*from the inside out.* Why did all this come about? Where did these influential people ever get the idea that, in the name of "doing good," they could change an individual's behavior by remaking the self, indeed, by "improving" the offenders' "character" with "moral guidance." What happened, I want to argue, was that forms of punishment and justice such as the public whipping post, like other "premodern" social practices, were swept away with the birth of the modern era. In order to understand the kind of disciplinary techniques we practice today, we need to understand them in historical context and this demands that we interrogate the very meaning of *modernity*.

THE BIRTH OF THE MODERN

The roots of modernity lie in the post-Renaissance period from the mid-sixteenth century until about the early 1800s, a period often referred to as the Enlightenment. From this age came a fundamental break from medieval tradition and religious dogmas. Unfettered by such constraints, the idea emerged that autonomous, universal, human "reason," not simply God's laws, would bring certainty, hope, and progress to the world. Indeed, the Enlightenment is credited with giving birth to a near-utopian vision of a future in which human emancipation and "enlightened" thinking would prevail. As these ideas and practices took hold, more traditional forms of social, economic, and cultural life began to crumble under the weight of changes in economic organization, scientific experimentation, and the rise of democratic states and rational law.

This movement intensified and culminated in the birth of the modern era—for our purposes, from around the turn of the nineteenth century and continuing through the first half of the twentieth century. We can summarize the main themes and characteristics of modernity as follows:

An increased rationalizing or calculating attitude toward social life based on notions of efficiency, predictability, control, and discipline—epitomized by the emergence of the factory and machine-based capitalism

The progressive differentiation of social life in the division of labor, specialization, and separation of the "public" and "private," "home" and "work" life, and the like

The rise of large-scale state and private organizations and bureaucracies as well as large, urban centers

The acceleration or "compression" of time-space relations—a fast-paced world that is made "smaller" by emerging modes of transportation and communication

The rise of a relatively large middle and professional class with it's own self-interest, sensibilities, and culture

The development of the "human sciences" such as psychology, psychiatry, sociology, criminology, demography, statistics, and the like

The institutionalization of the belief in progress, driven by the idea that scientific knowledge, objective reason, and technology could harness nature and could change social life and human existence for the better

Modernity's achievements were considerable. It gave birth to democratic movements in the West that increased personal freedoms and liberties for most, including minorities, women, and the propertyless classes. Governments regulated social relations and put in place rational systems of law, justice, monetary exchange, schooling, and social welfare systems. Driven by the dynamic and technology-based system of capitalism, transportation, communication, and utility systems proliferated, while literacy expanded and the standard of living increased as consumer goods became readily available. Scientific experimentation, medical discoveries, and public health and sanitation movements helped wipe out diseases and reduce various forms of human suffering.

Yet modernity has always had its detractors. Karl Marx (1818–1883) wrote about the devastating poverty, exploitation, and alienation that he saw in nineteenth-century capitalism. The French sociologist Émile Durkheim (1858–1917) considered how geographic and class mobility and the loss of tradition in culture were likely to produce a feeling of *anomie,* or normlessness, on the part of many. The German social scientist Max Weber (1864–1920) offered the view that modernity's distinctive "formal rationality"—as epitomized in large, bureaucratic organizations—represented an "iron cage" that would ultimately entrap us. And an even darker view is found in the writings of anti-Enlightenment philosopher Friedrich Nietzsche (1844–1900).

Nietzsche offered a direct challenge to the optimistic worldview of the Enlightenment and the so-called advances of modernity. For Nietzsche, this period's "progress," the discovery of absolute "Truths," and its scientific and technical "innovation" were more about what he called the *Will to Power:* the human drive to dominate nature and the environment. While Nietzsche praised the critical spirit of the Enlightenment, he disputed those who claimed to have discovered universal moral codes and systems of reason, since he believed that, given the diversity of human nature, such codes could not apply to everyone. This meant that those asserting lawlike standards must necessarily place themselves—morally, socially, and culturally—above others, thereby dominating them. It follows then that, from this perspective, the history of recent human experience is not a simple procession of higher universal morals and higher standards of reason. Rather, driven by the desire for some ultimate "Truth" and knowledge, humans have produced one system of domination after the other. (As it was once put, we "progressed" in the twentieth century, for example, from "the slingshot to the megaton bomb.") In this view, knowledge cannot be separated from power. The ideological system of Enlightenment reason, rationality, and progress is seen as just that: another ideology, another interpretation of reality, advanced by one group over others, rather than some ultimate, final, "Truth."

For Nietzsche, then, as well as for Weber and, later, for Foucault, the post-Enlightenment period is one of increasing *domination* masked in a guise of emancipation and humanitarianism. As one writer put it, "Awakening in the classical world like a sleeping giant, reason finds chaos and disorder everywhere and embarks on a rational ordering of the social, attempting to classify and regulate all forms of experience. . . ."[5] Foucault suggests that rather than a utopian dream of freedom, late-eighteenth-century politicians, philosophers, and jurists offered a blueprint for a military model of society in which discipline and self-control would become a central organizing theme. Uniform precision, bodily discipline, rigid hierarchies, and "the drill" designed to mold and shape the body become techniques of social control that are easily adapted beyond the military camps and hospitals where these techniques were discovered and perfected. The modern individual was born, according to Foucault, into a sea of regulations, petty rules and subrules, and fussy inspections, a world where the supervision of the smallest fragments of life and of the body takes place in the context of the school, the barracks, the hospital, and the workshop.[6]

The experiences that Foucault saw as the most vulnerable to rationalization, scientific inquiry, and official scrutiny were madness, criminality, poverty, forms of deviance, and even sexuality. With Enlightenment zeal, late-eighteenth-century *ideologues* turned their attention from the control of nature to the manipulation of "man" by way of the emerging knowledge of the "human sciences" such as psychology, neurology, psychiatry, sociology, criminology, demography, and the like. In other words, in new and important ways, human beings—our bodies, minds, and behaviors—became the *subject* of scientific inquiry and the *object* of its passions. The rise of the human sciences as a topic of inquiry, then, is closely linked with the emergence of new "disciplinary technologies" designed to treat the human body as an "object" to be broken down, analyzed, and improved. This is a crucial turn of events. Rather than focusing on dominating the world around them, late-Enlightenment scholars turned the *Will to Power* on the human race. Rational and scientific knowledge and discourses (that is, systems of language overlapping with cultural practices), along with bureaucratic organizations, provided the means to classify, regulate, exclude, and even eliminate any human behavior deemed outside an increasingly narrow definition of "normal." Some would argue that, say, Nazi Germany or Stalinist Russia were, rather than some aberration in the course of human progress, a natural outcome of the rational, calculating mind of modernity. As Foucault once said, both regimes "used and extended mechanisms already present in most other societies. More then that: in spite of their own internal madness, they used to a large extent the ideas and the devices of our political rationality."[7]

So, it would seem that this is the historical context of how we in the West got the idea that we could, regardless of an individual's particular "defect," reconstruct a more idealized person if only he or she could be subjected to the right disciplinary regime.

CASTLES OF OUR CONSCIENCE

Nowhere is this mentality and the emergence of the modern disciplinary institution more evident than in the United States.[8] In addition to their sudden revulsion to violence, what became clear to reformers in the late eighteenth and early nineteenth centuries was that the whipping post and the rack were a messy business and, increasingly, a political liability in postrevolutionary America. These inherited English criminal statutes were a constant reminder of monarchical political oppression, while those involving "cruel" sanctions were not applied consistently, making criminal justice arbitrary and ineffectual. In these early years, "A jury, squeezed between two distasteful choices, death or acquittal, often acquitted the guilty," according to Lawrence Friedman.[9] This kind of "jury lawlessness," often provoked vigilante justice, endangering the establishment of rational-legal authority and, therefore, the political power of the new government. A more predictable, orderly, and democratic set of punishments was needed to support the new political regime. We see, then, the emergence of a new discourse of crime and new forms of punishment.[10]

Inspired by the writings of the influential Italian criminologist Cesare Beccaria and his new "science of man," *Homo Criminalis,* as well as others, people like Dr. Benjamin Rush (1745–1813), who (from my perspective, ironically) was a signer of the Declaration of Independence, set out to reinvent criminal justice practice. This new discourse on crime and punishment was celebrated in a now-well-known set of principles:

1. Punishment must be as unarbitrary as possible.
2. Punishment should be a deterrent to future criminality.
3. There should be temporal modulation, since punishment can function only if it comes to an end.
4. Each crime and each penalty would be clearly laid out in a classification scheme.
5. The guilty should be only one of the targets of punishment, for punishment is directed above all at the potentially guilty.

The bodies of condemned offenders were now the property of society rather than of the king. Such ideas were infused with the notion of the social contract: that crime was an attack on society itself and that punishment should right the wrong done to the community and restore offenders to their proper places in it. Criminal justice would be rational not emotional, according to the reformers. It would approach the mind and soul of the criminal and not just the body.

For a while, it was deemed that performing public works was the best treatment for the offender. In Philadelphia, for example, the application of the city's "wheelbarrow" law of 1786 put shaven-headed, ragged, chain-gang prisoners to work cleaning the streets under the watchful eye of armed guards. But the sight of these men became increasingly distasteful to the good citizens of the city as the convicts went about "begging and insulting the inhabitants, [and] collecting crowds of idle boys," and they became the sport of others who tormented the prisoners incessantly. The law of March 27, 1789 soon sequestered prisoners to conditions of more "private" punishment at the Walnut Street jail.[11] Here the prisoners were subjected to a "moral" regime of solitary confinement, hard labor, diet control, and bodily hygiene. Yet not long after it was built, conditions at the jail deteriorated; jail inspectors began pardoning prisoners to alleviate overcrowding, abuses and neglect were exposed, and serious riots took place. The result was unanimous condemnation of the Walnut Street jail. Yet rather than scrap the experiment with incarceration, authorities pressed on and called for the building of new, larger, state penitentiaries. Undertaking the most ambitious public works program in Pennsylvania's history to date, the western and eastern facilities were erected by the laws of 1817 and 1821, marking the beginnings of Pennsylvania's prison "system." The situation was similar elsewhere, as other states increased their commitment to institutional punishment.

This turn to rationally organized, reformatory institutions and the new "science of man" influenced society's response to other behaviors as well. Before about 1825, the majority of poor and dependent people had been customarily cared for in noninstitutional ways. Those close to the center of town life might stay in their own homes with the help of the community, or they were placed with relatives, friends, or fellow church members. Those on the margins were "boarded" with townsfolk, with a widow for example, at a negotiated price. Later, communities made direct payments to people in their homes, while some able-bodied poor might be "auctioned off" to farmers and others and were put to work for their keep. Yet, after the 1820s, these apparently flexible and informal arrangements began to break down under the weight of expanded commercial development, the erosion of social cohesion in small towns, the attraction of wealth, and the increasing stratification of towns and villages. Townsfolk, particularly those of the middle and upper classes, became less willing to take in and board the increasing number of strangers and outsiders appearing in their area.

In New York, for example, an influential report by the secretary of state in 1824 estimated the total number of poor in New York to be 22,111 and the cost of providing for them to be close to $500,000. The report advocated the establishment of a system of county poorhouses modeled after the "House of Industry" which had been erected in Rensselaer county in 1820. The idea was that each inmate would work to his or her own ability as a means of stimulating industry and sharing the expense of their maintenance. These houses of employment would ideally be connected to a workhouse or penitentiary "for the reception and discipline of sturdy beggars and vagrants." Street beggary would be entirely prohibited. By 1835, almshouses appeared in 51 out of 54 state counties.

The principal advantages of the poorhouse seem clear. It isolated the dependent from the growing middle-class community, who increasingly considered the pauper an idler and troublemaker. Rather than have the indigent scattered around town in private dwellings or, worse yet, begging on street corners, the almshouse centralized relief administration and provided for more effective surveillance of their activities by one overseer. However, before long, the "new" system of county indoor relief was itself in crisis. For what was hailed as the final solution to dependency revealed itself as yet another administrative, jurisdictional, and financial mess. In New York, annual reports from throughout the state to the legislature uncovered shocking abuse of inmates. Idleness was pervasive, especially in the larger houses. Economic depressions between 1837 and 1843, and later between 1857 and 1858, combined with the dramatic increase in immigration, placed an incredible burden on relief agencies. State governments, grappling to gain some rational control over the system and expenditures, began to create central administrative agencies to coordinate the activities of public charities. Massachusetts was the first to create a state board of charities in 1863. Later that year, New York established its board. By 1873 boards had been set up in Illinois, Pennsylvania, North Carolina, Rhode Island, Michigan, Wisconsin, Kansas, and Connecticut.

One important development which followed the establishment of these state boards was the process of classifying and segregating the population of the almshouses and moving inmates into facilities designated for their particular "defect." Reformers contended that the care and control function of the poorhouse could be better served if each class of dependent had its own particular needs addressed, since the mixing of such classes had created conditions which were detrimental to all. This "classification" movement attempted to extend administrative rationality and planning by isolating each particular class of deviants and dependents, not only to physically separate them from each other but also to gain more effective surveillance, observation, and control. Gender, age, and mental and physical capacities were the basis of boundaries among the new facilities, which prevented, through the restriction of both social and sexual contact, the procreation of the "defective classes." Second, once so isolated, each facility could engage in a more exacting process of distinguishing the degree of each class's "rehabilitative" potential. Whereas custodial care was all that could be expected for the very old, the very young, the infirm, or the completely helpless, others, including recalcitrant children, the healthy deviant, the slightly feeble and the like, could be educated and trained to labor both inside and, eventually, outside the institution.

The first group of dependents affected by the movement for separation was the insane. By 1881, there were six state hospitals for the acutely and chronically insane in New York, for example. Between 1850 and 1869, thirty-five new hospitals were opened in other states, and, by 1890, fifty-nine others came into existence, with the post-1870 hospitals increasingly larger in size. Children were similarly drawn away from the mixed almshouse where they were, for the most part, "badly fed, badly clothed, badly taken care of, and exposed to the degrading influence of those in immediate charge of them," according to reformer Louisa Lee Schuyler. Specialized juvenile correction facilities—houses of refuge, reformatories, and training schools—expanded both the classification scheme and the system of care and control of dependent and troublesome children. Not only were children increasingly institutionalized in segregated facilities, but the legal mechanisms by which they got there changed as well. The juvenile court represented one more manifestation of the increasingly bureaucratic system of social control and the trend toward administrative reform and rationality; within twenty-five years of the adoption of the first juvenile court legislation, in Illinois in 1899, courts were established in every state but two. While perhaps more ceremonial than substantive at first, the juvenile court evolved to possess broad-sweeping jurisdiction over the lives of children under the age of 16. The court's ideological foundation rested on the notion of *parens patriae,* or "parental care," and thus the legal institution was charged with protecting and providing for the needs of delinquent, dependent, and neglected youth.

The darker side of the reform story, however, was the regulation of family life by the state along with few alternatives to an institutional response to youthful misconduct. By 1940, juvenile courts in the United States handled 200,000 delinquency cases alone, not including the dependent and neglected—a rate of 10.5 per 1,000 of those between the ages of

10 and 17. By 1955, the corresponding figures were 431,000 cases with a rate of 21.4 per 1,000. In comparing figures from the U.S. Bureau of the Census for juvenile correctional facilities between 1923 and 1950, we see that these populations rose from 27,238 in 1923; to 30,496 in 1933; and to 40,880 by 1950. The corresponding rates per 100,000 of those in the population under age 18 were 65.7, 72.3, and 88.8, respectively.

Specialized facilities were also developed for the "feebleminded" and the epileptic. "Mental defectives" were further classified as "teachable" or "unteachable." Concerned with the "hereditary factor" in the proliferation of crime, pauperism, and mental deficiency, reformers and state welfare administrators sought to isolate its source, which, according to one reformer, was "the unrestrained liberty allowed to vagrant and degraded women." They urged the creation of an institution for "vagrant and degraded" women which, if not reformation, could at least cut off the line of pauper descendants. In New York, the campaign resulted in 1887 in the House of Refuge for Women at Hudson, where "all females between the ages of fifteen and thirty years who have been convicted of petty larceny, habitual drunkenness, of being common prostitutes, frequenters of disorderly houses or houses of prostitution" were to be placed. Suitable employment was to be provided, which would encourage "habits of self supporting industry" and "mental and moral improvement." This facility was soon filled to capacity, and three other women's reformatories were erected in the state by the late 1890s.

So, from the view I want to take here, the inventions of the penitentiary, the poorhouse, and the mental asylum were not simply chapters in a long humanitarian crusade. Driven by ideas having their origins in Enlightenment reason and progressive faith, a constellation of influential philosophers, jurists, reformers, and state authorities aided in *the creation and expansion of a system of social control for modern society not possible in the premodern, Classical Age.* Ironically then, it might be argued that, in the name of "humanity" and "emancipation," reformers created *more* formal social control, not less. Reformers, interested in punishing more effectively and more certainly, went beyond the surface of the skin, into the very heart and soul of the deviant. In doing so, they approached the criminal, the deviant, and the poor as an object to be manipulated, whereas just a short time before, the community had confronted the "impenitent sinner" deserving of corporal punishment or, in the case of the poor, simply a person who had been "reduced to want."

Under the authority of the state and "in the name of the people," these reformers—increasingly middle and professional class—asserted a new system of universal "moral" principles and a new discourse on crime and punishment that placed themselves as "experts" and authorities—increasingly trained in the human sciences—at the center of justice practice. Reflecting the central themes of modernity, disorderly and ill-defined forms of public torture and stigmatization ceremonies were replaced by rationally organized legal codes as well as reformatory institutions such as prisons, poorhouses, and asylums that this new social class would run and supervise. Rather than seek retribution, they removed punishment from public view and placed it behind the walls of the institution. The "dangerous rogue," sent away to places like Auburn, was subjected to a secular, military-like apparatus that would transform him or her into a newly defined democratic subject: "A diligent, literate laborer. A moderate, self-interested citizen."[12] And, as I have shown, it was soon asserted that the poor could be made "industrious," the deviant turned from deviant ways, and the insane brought back to reason. Listen to these notions in the words of some of these early reformers:

> You take a *child;* you must not expect to make her, without care, and instruction and patience, a useful domestic. Encourage what you may find good in her, and in punishing her faults, consider how you should endeavor to correct those of your own children.
> —Boston Children's Aid Society, *Reminiscences of the Boston Female Orphan Asylum* (1844)

> To make a vagrant efficient is more praiseworthy than to make two blades of grass grow where one grew before.
> —E. Stagg Whitin, *Penal Servitude* (1912)

> Outside the walls a man must choose between work and idleness—between honesty and crime. Why not teach him these lessons before he comes out?
> —Thomas Mott Osborne, *Society and Prisons* (1916)

DISCIPLINE AS A TECHNIQUE

The modern era, therefore, gave birth to a range of techniques and practices that were designed to mold and shape the body as well as the mind. These practices involve a distinctly modern form of social and political constraint that Michel Foucault called "disciplinary power." This kind of power is thought of as a technique that is *exercised* rather than as a commodity that is *held.* This is a radical alternative to traditional sociological conceptions of power. Most theories assert that power lies in the hands of the "powerful" who control social resources, for example, the owners of capital or political elites. "Power" is often assumed to emanate—somewhat mysteriously I might add—from these resources. Additionally, these theories often neglect to consider the relationship between power and knowledge, taking for granted that knowledge is either politically neutral or necessarily liberating. Such "resource" theories of power may be important in understanding, say, the perpetuation of social classes. Unfortunately, they are often "reductionistic" in that they reduce all forms of social power to class domination or to the more "macro" structures of the economy, political authority, or the state. In doing so, they may tell us very little about the more "micro" level—the concrete ways in which individuals, their bodies and behaviors, are controlled and shaped in everyday life. The exercise of "discipline" may augment, and may even be intimately bound up with, other forms of political, social, and economic power, but it cannot be simply subsumed by them.

Disciplinary power, then, is thought of as being "bi-directional," not simply operating from the "top down" but circulating throughout the social body. That is, it does not necessarily flow directly from the highest levels of the government, or from ruling elites simply imposed on the masses, but may be developed and practiced by a wide range of people in a host of institutional sites. So rather than being concentrated in the hands of a few, disciplinary power appears nearly everywhere, dispersed and fragmented. In this view, we are all involved and enmeshed within a matrix of power relations that are highly intentional and purposeful; arrangements that can be more or less unequal but are never simply one directional. Some examples: Consider the proliferation of drug testing programs in the workplace and the cases of Samuel Allen and Daryl Kenyon. Allen is a highly paid president of the international division of a large corporate sporting-goods store with more than ten thousand employees. Kenyon, on the other hand, works on the production line at a large office-furniture manufacturer. Despite their obvious differences in resources, status, and authority, both men were required to offer hair samples to be tested for drugs when they were hired. Both men even consent to this form of surveillance by endorsing the programs in their companies.[13] Or think of the police. While they can exercise considerable authority over the citizenry, they must, however, in order to function legitimately, discipline themselves with bureaucratic rules and regulations, a rigid hierarchy of command, and the close monitoring and evaluation of each other's actions.

The exercise of disciplinary power is often continuous, automatic, and anonymous (think of the surveillance video camera, for example). It is extensive and thorough, and it is capillary as well, meaning that it extends out to the remotest corners of society. It disciplines individuals efficiently and effectively, with the least amount of physical force, labor power, and expense. Knowledge, in Foucault's scheme, is intrinsic to the spread and proliferation of disciplinary power. Knowledge is not equal to power, nor is power the same as knowledge; each presupposes the other. Again, consider drug testing. Such tests are a disciplinary ritual that uses scientific knowledge *of* the body to derive knowledge *from* the body. This information is then used as the basis to judge and/or to take action against an individual. Without knowledge, power cannot be exercised without force; without the authority to punish, the knowledge or evidence is meaningless.

Finally, disciplinary power is often productive and not simply repressive. This is an important point. If disciplinary power operated in a despotic fashion, it would meet with far more resistance. Instead of dominating with force and oppression, proponents stress the obvious productive benefits from various disciplinary techniques, thus appeasing opposition. The techniques of disciplinary power are "corrective," and proponents may employ rewards or privileges to accomplish the goal of modifying behavior. For example, supervision in a workshop may have been set up to avoid theft, but the knowledge gathered from the monitoring may also be used to enhance employees' skills and productivity. In such a case, workers are encouraged to use the company's surveillance system to their own advantage by becoming "better" workers. Suspected substance users are taught to use the company's random drug tests to keep themselves "clean," while "motivated" students are persuaded to utilize a teacher's tracking system to meet goals and complete their work.

So it is during the modern era that, according to Foucault, a variety of these relatively modest disciplinary procedures were perfected by the doctors, wardens, and schoolmasters of the new institutions. It was these individuals who were the first to confront problems of managing large numbers of people in confined spaces. With the help of the knowledge of the emerging human sciences, they devised detailed, micro methods for the efficient supervision and surveillance of inmates in order to produce obedience and conformity. These methods include strict posture and machinelike movements such as in the "lockstep"-and-silence system; monotonous uniforms; the separation and classification of people by their diseases, abilities, and the like; orderly lines of desks so one teacher can observe the entire room; and even the smallest architectural details, such as large dividers between bathroom stalls to prevent sexual misconduct.

The control of time and space was crucial in these institutions; every minute of every day and every activity of the inmates were monitored and scheduled. Enclosure permitted the division of internal space into an orderly grid where, as Foucault put it, "each individual has his own place; and each place its individual." It was in these closed, disciplinary organizations where, for the first time, people were treated as "cases" about whom authorities attempted to build extensive dossiers including life histories, family backgrounds, and rehabilitative progress. There were also series of micro penalties established to scan conduct and ensure social control. Offenses such as lateness, absences, inattention, impoliteness, disobedience, poor attitude, and lack of cleanliness were subjected to light physical punishments, minor deprivations, and petty humiliations. By specifying the most minute details of every day, disciplinary power makes almost any behavior punishable and thus the object of attention, surveillance, and control.

Disciplinary power is further enhanced by the use of more general procedures such as "the examination." This is a ritualized knowledge-gathering activity in which case files are built out of the often-mundane details of people's lives and activities. Two key elements are used to build these files: "Hierarchical observation" involves surveillance, information collection, and analysis as a central organizing principal of the institution. Disciplining individuals through observation requires the delegation of supervision. Here individuals carry out the act of watching others while they themselves are being watched. "Normalizing judgments" entail the assessment of an individual's activity set against some standard or ideal where all behavior lies between two poles, "good" and "bad," and can be judged—with small, graduated distinctions—along the continuum. Foucault argued that the goal of these procedures was to forge what he called "docile" bodies: mute, obedient individuals who have been subjected, transformed, and improved.

This notion of docility is very important to the ideas presented in this book, for it is the ultimate aim of most forms of social control. The opposite of docility is rebellious, wild, and disagreeable behavior. Robert Emerson and Sheldon Messinger refer to the "politics of trouble" when they point out that most behavior that comes to be labeled "deviant," problematic, or disagreeable originates with people causing "trouble" for others or by feeling troubled themselves.[14] No matter what its stated purpose—to "help," "cure," "punish," or "rehabilitate"—social control that is aimed at the juvenile delinquent, the unemployed, the mentally ill, the nursing-home resident, or the recalcitrant worker is intended to render that individual manageable, submissive, teachable, tractable, and pliable. The "politics of trouble" are echoed in the commands "Keep in line," "Don't talk back," "Eat your dinner," "Don't make noise," "Don't cause problems," "Work harder," and so on.

BENTHAM'S *PANOPTICON*

Amid the array of modern disciplinary practices, Foucault chose to highlight what he considered to be an exemplar in the operation of modern disciplinary technology: the *Panopticon*. In 1791, British utilitarian philosopher, economist, and jurist Jeremy Bentham (1748–1832) printed a collection of letters he had written to a friend under the long-winded yet informative title of *Panopticon; or, The Inspection- House: Containing the Idea of a New Principle of Construction Applicable to any Sort of Establishment, in Which Persons of any Description are to be Kept Under Inspection; and Particular to Penitentiary-Houses, Prisons, Poor-Houses, Lazarettos, Houses of Industry, Manufactories, Hospitals, Work-Houses, Mad-Houses, and Schools with A Plan of Management Adapted to the Principle*. The detailed architectural design for the Panopticon called for the construction of a building with a central tower that contained the "inspector's lodge." Around the lodge, in a circular form, was a set of peripheral cells with windows in the rear and front of each cell so that, in effect, the cell space was back-lit. The prisoner (lunatic, schoolboy, etc.) could then be subjected to the constant observation of the person occupying the lodge. Bentham himself anticipated the "politics of trouble" when he emphasized that the goal of docility could be easily achieved with the Panopticon design, "[n]o matter how different or opposite the purpose: whether it be that of punishing the incorrigible, guarding the insane, reforming the vicious, confining the suspected, employing the idle, maintaining the helpless, curing the sick, [or] instructing the willing. . . ."

The Panopticon reversed the principles of the dungeon; it was about light and visibility rather than darkness and isolation. Yet the prisoners would be kept in the dark, in another sense, as the lodge would be constructed with an elaborate venetian-blind effect that Bentham called the "inspector's lantern": a sort of one-way mirror that masked the presence or absence of an observer. Bentham created this device because, according to his very efficient plans, the inspector would also function as the institution's bookkeeper. Yet if he performed this task, his lamp would give away his presence to the inmates. So Bentham designed the lantern so that the only thing the inmates could see was a dark spot at the center of the aperture. With this scheme, the inmates are not really under constant surveillance; they just think or imagine that they are. As Bentham put it, they are "awed to silence by an invisible eye." The inmates have therefore internalized what Foucault called *le regard*, or the "gaze" of the authorities, and, in effect, they watch and render *themselves* docile. In this way, power operates without force or violence, automatically and continuously, whether or not the tower is occupied at all. With this technology, Bentham created an all-seeing, all-knowing "God" that was, in reality, nothing more than a dark spot in the lantern. In Bentham's words, "in a Panopticon the inspector's back is never turned." And he asserted the productive benefits of his design for the "inspection-house"

in the opening lines of his treatise: "Morals reformed—health preserved—industry invigorated—instruction diffused—public burdens
lightened . . .—all by a simple idea in architecture!"[15]

While the design for the Panopticon was never adopted in its pure
form, many of its principles were deployed, and it stimulated considerable discussion and new techniques for social control. But the fact that it
had limited direct impact did not diminish its importance, Foucault
argued. Its significance lay *in the very idea* that such a design was thought
to be necessary or desirable at the time. The Panopticon remains both an
important symbol of modern disciplinary technology and a basic principle on which many forms of contemporary surveillance operate (for
example, the rotating video cameras on school buses that I mentioned in
Chapter 1).

THE "SWARMING OF
DISCIPLINARY MECHANISMS"

Let me summarize Foucault's contribution to our understanding of
modern social control. Influenced by a radical critique of Enlightenment
reason, Foucault chose to study the relationships among *experiences* such
as madness and criminality, the *knowledge* produced by the new "sciences
of man," and the manner in which *power* was exercised on bodies and
"souls" through "meticulous rituals" in institutions like asylums and
penitentiaries. It was in those institutions that he saw the fullest realiza-
tion of the military model of society emerging in the modern era. In
other words, life in the penitentiary, reformatory, and poorhouses represented an idealized version of a utopian, bourgeois society: a machinelike, disciplined culture, set on obedience, order, and uniformity. The
shaping, molding, and construction of "docile bodies" would be accom-
plished through the use of various "disciplinary technologies." These
techniques ranged from the "lockstep" to ritualistic examinations with
their "hierarchical observations" designed to instill the "gaze" of authorities and produce self-control, and "normalizing judgments" that set the
behavioral standards to be upheld.

In *Discipline and Punish*, Foucault set out the "early" modern origins
of disciplinary power within the confines of closed, disciplinary institutions. Yet this is only the beginning, as he quite clearly anticipated postmodern developments. "While on the one hand," he states, "the disciplinary establishments increase, their mechanisms have a certain tendency
to become 'de-institutionalized,' to emerge from the closed fortresses in
which they once functioned and to circulate in the 'free' state; the massive, compact disciplines are broken down into flexible methods of con-

trol, which may be transferred and adapted."[16] He calls this the "swarm-ing of disciplinary mechanisms." Here he means that micro disciplinary techniques that were developed in the institutions began to reach out from those organizations, linking up with other institutions and prac-tices, creating a more macro web of social control. For example, schools begin to supervise the conduct of the parents as well as of the children, the hospital monitors the patients in addition to the other inhabitants of the district, and relief officials "oversee" not just the poor but their entire extended families as well. Remember, disciplinary power is capillary; it expands out, colonizes, and moves to the tiniest reaches of social life. Once this happens, we have a society where everyday life is increasingly filled with "meticulous rituals of power" involving surveillance, exami-nations, and knowledge-gathering activities. This creates, according to Foucault, "A subtle, graduated, carceral net, with compact institutions, but also separate and diffused methods" which he sees as far more effec-tive than the "arbitrary, widespread, badly integrated" practices of the classical age.[17] We see, then, "an increasing ordering in all realms under the guise of improving the welfare of the individual and the population. . . . [T]his order reveals itself as a strategy, with no one directing it and everyone increasingly enmeshed in it, whose only end is the increase of power and order itself."[18]

In Foucault's account, the foundation of this kind of "disciplinary" society was in place in Europe as early as the seventeenth century. I believe that it has only been in the last half of the twentieth century, at least in the United States, that we are witnessing the historical movement from *excep-tional* punishment—that is, the disciplining of a particular individual for committing a particular offense—to the *generalized* surveillance of us all. I want to argue here that the conditions that constituted modern social control practices are changing and that new disciplinary technologies and discourses are taking hold. In short, I believe we are witnessing the emer-gence of a new regime of discipline and social control—a regime that retains many of the modern themes and practices of the past, while, at the same time, is both a product and a reflection of contemporary *post*mod-ern culture. Therefore I believe there exists today an increasing tension between two practices of social control. As Foucault put it:

> At one extreme, the . . . enclosed institution, established
> on the edges of society . . . arresting evil, breaking com-
> munications, suspending time. At the other extreme . . .
> the discipline-mechanism: a functional mechanism that
> *must improve the exercise of power by making it lighter,*
> *more rapid, more effective, a design of subtle coercion for*
> *a society yet to come.* (Emphasis mine)[19]

THE POSTMODERN MOMENT

It seems clear that we have witnessed, in the post–World War II period (and more intensely since the early 1970s), significant changes in the organization of Western society and culture. Some social theorists think that these changes reflect an "exhaustion" of modernity and signal the beginning of a new, "postmodern" period of history. Most scholars would acknowledge that this transition is happening while many "modern" institutions and practices remain in place. Just what are these conditions that make up postmodernity? We best see the characteristics by comparing them with the dimensions of modernity I offered earlier; see Table 2-1.

As I indicated in Chapter 1, ours is a culture deeply penetrated by commodities and consumer "lifestyles." Generated by corporate marketing strategies, from Eddie Bauer to J. Crew, from Infiniti automobiles to the latest "concept" in chain restaurants, companies sell us images of how we want to see ourselves as much as they market products. As Donald Lowe puts it, most of us in "late capitalism USA" "no longer consume commodities to satisfy relatively stable and specific needs, but to reconstruct ourselves in terms of the lifestyles associated with the consumption of certain commodities."[20] The economic viability of America is now in the hands of our willingness to purchase these prized lifestyle insignias, where, for most of us, time spent in work has become little more than a means to fulfill what is now defined as our near-patriotic duty to consume. And when we do go to work, it may be to a "virtual" company that "flexibly" hires consultants for its labor force, "outsources" its manufacturing needs, and changes its organizational structure like a chameleon.

Increasingly, time and social and geographical space are highly compressed by rapidly changing communication, computer technologies, and information storage and retrieval. We have, at the click of a mouse button, access to vast amounts of information, but many may not have a clue about how to make sense of it. We can "surf" the virtual globe of the Internet but not know or seemingly care who sits on our own city council. And we may have a cable television network that can bring us unlimited "entertainment," but we may find that, as the title of one Bruce Springsteen song suggests, there are "57 channels (and nothin' on)." Each day brings us startling scientific and medical knowledge that, as Vaclav Havel, the playwright and president of the Czech Republic, stated, "can explain anything in the objective world to us, yet we understand our own lives less and less. We live in a postmodern world, were almost anything is possible and nothing is certain."[21]

TABLE 2-1

CHARACTERISTICS OF MODERNITY AND POSTMODERNITY

Modernity	Postmodernity
Rationalization of social life epitomized by the rigid predictability and control of the factory and machine-based capitalism (Fordism).	"Flexible" movements in use of labor, manufacturing organization, markets, products, organizational innovation, and "service" economy (post-Fordism).
Division of labor, specialization, and clear separation of the "public" and "private," gender roles, home and work life, and the like. Relatively stable nation-state boundaries and hierarchy and colonialism.	Blurring of boundaries. Implosion of once-taken-for-granted meanings, symbols, and institutions of modern life: work, marriage, family, health, sexuality, intimacy, gender, privacy, etc. This is often combined with a nostalgia for the past. Shifting global boundaries and power centers and decolonialization.
Rise of large-scale, centralized state and private organizations and bureaucracies as well as urban space.	Increasing decentralization, e.g., public housing, community "corrections" and "policing," public schools, corporate divisions, and suburbanization.
"Compression" of time-space relations. Fast-paced world made "smaller" by new modes of transportation and communication.	Intensified time-space compression creating intense disorientation and disruption in cultural and social life. A dominant video culture; the commodification of sexuality and desire and a celebration of consumer lifestyles.
Large middle and professional class with its own self-interest, sensibilities, and culture. It becomes the dominant cultural definition, culminating in the 1950s.	Increasing challenges to middle-class "nuclear family" from women, gays, ethnic and religious groups, as well as cultural diversity with acknowledged "different voices."
Rise of the "human sciences" modeled after the physical sciences aimed at "knowable man" through individuality, consciousness, and behavior.	Collapse of "grand narratives" and a turn away from the scientific approach to society; rise of feminist, cultural studies agenda that takes gender, class, race, and ethnicity to be central to any analysis of society.
Utopian belief in progress, driven by the idea that scientific knowledge, objective reason, and technology could harness nature and change social life and human existence for the better.	Increasing skepticism about progress and of those who assert its possibility; criticism of scientific knowledge and rationality.

This uncertainty is exacerbated by the blurring of boundaries between the once-taken-for-granted meanings, symbols, and institutions of modern life such as work, marriage, family, health, sexuality, intimacy, gender, privacy, etc. An underlying anxiety may be created from our increasing inability to distinguish "fact" from fiction and the "real" from the "simulation of the real." Some argue that the "language of the visual," or "videocy," is rapidly replacing modern forms of literacy based on oral and written traditions. Within the flood of images presented in the mass media, how do we separate "investigative journalism" from "docudramas," *Real Cops* from the O. J. Simpson "slow-speed" chase, or "live" CNN coverage of the latest international skirmish from a cable show about advanced weaponry? In this context, authenticity begins to lose its anchoring points. Importantly, since such chaotic media have become our primary source of cultural knowledge, we often believe that we know and understand the world simply because we "saw it in the movies." This society, according to one theorist, only knows itself through the its own reflection in the camera's eye and through experience that may be replaced by its visual representation. Another suggests that television/video has a unique ability to break down the distinction between "here and there, live and mediated, personal and public" and has thus severed the links between social and physical space. This leads to a sense of "placelessness."[22] I was startled, for example, when one of my white, middle-class, University of Kansas students told me that he liked the film *Boyz N the Hood.* "Why?" I asked. He stated confidently, "Because it was like real life in South Central LA." Yet he has never been to South Central—never mind having lived there—and, in fact, has no frame of reference to compare the "real" to this fictional portrayal.

What effect do these conditions have on the way we experience life and how we interact with others? Norman Denzin argues that the ingredients of the postmodern self,

> are filtered through the personal troubles and the emotional experiences that flow from the individual's interactions with everyday life. . . . The raw economic, racial, and sexual edges of contemporary life produce anxiety, alienation, a radical isolation from others, madness, violence, and insanity. Large cultural groupings (young women, the elderly, racial and ethnic minorities, gays and lesbians) are unable either to live out their ideological versions of the American dream or to experience personal happiness. . . . Self-hatred, anger, envy, false self-pride, and a desire for revenge against the other are experienced. Sexism, racism, and homophobia are the undersides of resentment.[23]

The media(ted) culture of postmodern society has a tremendous effect on our ability to make informed political and policy decisions. Video journalists, sensational talk-show hosts, and those behind slick marketing campaigns have become, according to Denzin, the new "intellectuals" and "historians" who hold a near monopoly on the presentation and interpretation of politics and social issues and problems. Increasingly they have turned everyday life into a theatrical drama where the most compelling stories are those that recount lives filled with uncertainty and unpredictability. They point to the next burgeoning "crisis" that threatens to make you or me its latest victim: your daughter may be a drug user, your ex-husband a child molester, or your study partner a rapist.

My point is *not* to suggest that these problems are simply illusions. Rather my argument is that what may actually be a very rare occurrence is easily sensationalized into a widespread "social problem," creating fear and mistrust and distorting our ability to make informed political decisions. For example, as a parent, I find myself hesitating to leave my child at a city park, as I have nightmares of his picture ending up on a milk carton. Yet, despite the reported thousands of missing children each year publicized by a Washington-based lobbying group, the number of kids taken by strangers is actually extremely small. While even one kidnapping is obviously a tragedy, most missing children either are teenage runaways or are snatched by a parent in a messy divorce. Look closely at the fear campaigns of organizations such as the Partnership for a Drug-Free America that ask you to pick out the "drug dealer" from a full-page newspaper ad of laughing, squeaky-clean, white, middle-class, preadolescents. As the "director of creative development" (I love that title!) for the group has stated about the ads, "They are not pretty. They are not nice. They are not polite. They are designed to disturb and upset people."[24] Or think of the sensational case of accusations of child molestation at a preschool that results in teachers throughout the country not even daring—or even being allowed—to give a child a hug. Do we challenge the politician who claims that homicidal teenage "superpredators" are stalking the streets of America, when, in reality, 80 percent of the counties in the country in 1995 did not register a single homicide by a juvenile?

As the new purveyors of "truth" have gone about constructing the "reality" of epidemic crime and drug use, the disintegration of the nuclear family, or the laziness of homeless men and "cheating" welfare mothers, they have helped create a nostalgia for the "good ol' days" (that likely never existed). This lamenting for an ideal past became the platform of the New Right as it captured political power in the 1980s and has retained it in the 1990s. A coalition of right-wing politicians and religious fundamentalists began to (re)construct their version of the ideal citizen who personified the sacred values of religion, hard work, health, and self-reliance. This agenda was aided by both "New Democrats" claiming to be tough on crime, drugs, and welfare "dependency," as well as "liberals" who were willing to use the power of the state to enforce programmatic solutions to these "new" social problems. We therefore began a far-reaching campaign to regulate not only the traditional crimes of person and property but also the behaviors, conditions, and "lifestyles" of substance (ab)use, alcohol consumption, "eating disorders," tobacco consumption, sexuality, sexual promiscuity and "deviance," teenage pregnancy, out-of-marriage births, domestic violence, child abuse, "dysfunctional" families, various psychological or psychiatric disorders and other medical conditions such as "attention deficit disorder," and such diseases as AIDS.

And yet, we see, at the same time, a rejection of the practicality and effectiveness of modern institutions where "nothing works" and where "rehabilitation" is a waste of time and money. In our day, the prison has a diminished capacity to summon images of moral redemption and discipline. Not only does the ideology of reformation no longer conceal the reality of daily life on the inside, but the gaze of television and the cinema has taken us inside the asylum, offering us a drama of hopelessness and chaos. As a result of this attempt to regulate and control more and more of social life—as well as our increasing pessimism about institutional reform—we have turned to new "meticulous rituals" of social control that are being integrated into preexisting modern institutions and practices. Rather than isolating the body *from everyday* life for surveillance and control, these new techniques impose a structure and accountability on an individual's behavior and "lifestyle" *in the everyday*. And these new methods are often premised on regulating, probing, or measuring the body's functions, processes, characteristics, or movements. In other words, more and more "surveillance ceremonies" are taking place in our daily lives, and these are often based on assessing evidence and gaining knowledge from our bodies.

"JUST SAY NO" AND GONZO JUSTICE

The essentials of America's contemporary moral panic are best illustrated by the almost obsessional focus of the "war on drugs" that was set in motion in the late 1980s. As has been pointed out, "The Reagan-Bush administrations . . . needed a way to redefine American social control policies in order to further their broader political aims. . . . Substance abuse was the problem they decided upon."[25] Here we saw a public discourse that held the defective character of the individual drug user

responsible for nearly all the ills of contemporary society and helped justify a new politics of repression. This political agenda was underwritten
by strategically cutting federally sponsored community mental health
programs while allocating massive funds for a growing "substance abuse"
sector.[26] Restrictive plea bargaining and longer, determinate sentences
for drug-related offenses soon overwhelmed the country's courts, jails,
prisons, and probation and parole departments and sent authorities
searching for new ways to control drug-arrest populations.[27] Within the
swirl of the "crisis," our video culture brought us publicity stunts, or
what David Altheide calls "gonzo justice," such as the Los Angeles Police
department's use of a "battering ram," mounted on a military tank, to
crash into suspected (and sometimes mistaken) crack-cocaine houses.[28]

Yet while such media spectacles held public attention, authorities
were quietly introducing new disciplinary techniques, administered
through an evolving network of local, public and private substance abuse
and "community corrections" bureaucracies, and in what I will describe
in Chapter 3 as "intensive supervision programs." Supported by state
subsidies to local agencies, these programs are intended to divert prison-
bound, nonviolent felons from state institutions (a tactic known as
"deinstitutionalization"). It was argued that these individuals are "better
off" in the community, since they are "free" to participate as "productive"
members of society. Yet I contend that this movement has simply insert-
ed the power to judge and punish more deeply into the daily life of the
community, "deinstitutionalizing" not so much the offender but the disciplinary procedures and mechanisms of the prison. Once individuals
become enmeshed in these organizational webs, their bodies, behaviors,
movements, and actions can be monitored and controlled through a
structure of bureaucratic accountability and disciplinary rituals such as
drug testing, electronic monitoring, curfews, "surprise" work visits, and
the like.

Given the "intensity" of these kinds of programs, haven't we then
moved the disciplinary mechanism of the prison—the "gaze" of authorities, the surveillance, the judgments, the case files—into the community?[29] And having done so, haven't we blurred the boundary between the
modern, penal institution and the everyday life of the postmodern?
Politicians, the public, and even the "clients" may think that such programs are "better" than doing time in prison (which, of course, was supposed to be "better" than public torture), but, again, what standard is
being used to make these claims? Foucault argued that the enclosure of
institutions permitted the control of time and space that was essential for
the effective and efficient application of disciplinary power. It created an
orderly "grid" that placed each inmate in a visible square of light. I argue,
and will illustrate in the following chapters, that such a grid is being built

in the community. Here, the exercise of power is local and decentralized, methodical, and nearly automatic, as it is set within a framework of bureaucratic rules and regulations. Computers and telecommunication devices evoke the "gaze" of the state, while the body is monitored for evidence of deviant activity. Remaining "in the community" also integrates the deviant into—some would say "puts them under the control of"—the primary role of consumption in the society. To argue then that the emergence of new disciplinary practices are rooted in the postmodern is not to suggest that "modern" institutions or practices we have inherited will disappear anytime soon. After all, we are still incarcerating people at an unprecedented rate. Rather then replacements, these new applications should be seen as extensions of disciplinary power that invest, colonize, and link up preexisting forms. I will describe this process in more detail in Chapter 3.

But what do programs for convicted felons have to do with the rest of us? I want to argue that there are certain consequences for our society and culture as a whole that stem from recent program changes. Foucault tells us to look to judicial practice to observe changing attitudes about discipline and social control in other spheres of society. In studying modern social control he saw, for example, important similarities between the rational organization and monotonous routine of prison life and the shop floor of the new factories. Today, I argue, programs like "community corrections" tend to normalize the presence of formal social control in everyday life. Such a presence—even though it initially may target people in the justice system—raises our tolerance for social control. When combined with the rampant fear and mistrust generated by the media, the consequence is that we are more willing to condone, even insist, that we adopt more and more disciplinary practices and drills that soon become routine and commonplace. For example, drug screening had been well established in the community corrections system before the Supreme Court ruled that, even without probable cause, *any* student participating in public school athletics could be randomly tested. Likewise, with the emergence of community-based "electronic monitoring" of convicted felons, we also see that employers are tethering employees to "beepers" or monitoring their activities with video cameras, computer terminals, handheld data-entry tablets, or other forms of electronic surveillance "leashes." While prisons have armed guards, metal detectors, and video surveillance cameras, so does the Sunrise Multiplex movie theater in Valley Stream, New York, and so does Mount View High School in West Virginia. These parallels are too significant to ignore.

Even prisons themselves "blend in" to everyday life as they are made indistinguishable from other community institutions. In Lockhart, Texas, a small factory no different from the others on Industrial

Boulevard makes computer circuit boards and air conditioners. Its 138 "employees" are actually inmates doing time in the medium-security prison run by Wackenhut Corrections Corp.[30] Other facilities are designed to simulate suburban, high-tech industrial parks and often are referred to as "campuses." In Los Angeles, neighborhood-based, privately run "microprisons" holding illegal immigrants look no different from the surrounding apartment complexes—all of them have locked gates and bars on the windows. Meanwhile, in downtown Los Angeles, the Metropolitan Detention Center appears to be just another skyscraper or luxury hotel to those who drive by it everyday. In this facility, "guards" sport preppy blue blazers as they ride elevators from floor-to-floor. As one inmate told author Mike Davis, "Can you imagine the mind fuck of being locked up in a Holiday Inn?"[31] In fact, in California, where more money is now spent to keep people behind bars than is spent on higher education, some institutions are no longer called prisons at all; they have names like "Vacaville Medical Facility."

So, in the chapters that follow, I will be drawing on examples from and moving back and forth between the official justice system and the everyday life of the postmodern. In doing so, I will illustrate how the lines between these two spheres of social life are increasingly blurred by the use of new disciplinary practices and technologies. I will show how these new meticulous rituals of power are constituted by and indicative of conditions of postmodernity, and I will employ the ideas and concepts developed by Michel Foucault and other postmodern theorists to help us understand these developments. In Chapter 3, I will focus on new forms of surveillance that systematically watch and monitor our bodies and behaviors. I will show how our communities, homes, schools, and workplaces are increasingly infused with meticulous rituals and surveillance ceremonies.

NOTES

1. Alice Morse Earle, *Curious Punishments of Bygone Days.* Rutland, Vt.: Charles E. Tenant, 1972: 144–45.
2. W. David Lewis, *From Newgate to Dannemora.* Ithaca, N.Y.: Cornell University Press, 1975: 117–20.
3. It should also be pointed out that the "birth of the prison" did not end physical punishment. Inmates at penitentiaries, mental asylums, and poorhouses as well as children in houses of refuge and reformatories were subjected to systematic corporal punishment and physical and mental abuse, to say nothing of various "treatments." See David Rothman, *The Discovery of the Asylum: Social*

Order and Disorder in the New Republic. Boston: Little, Brown, 1971. Also see his *Conscience and Convenience: The Asylum and Its Alternatives in Progressive America.* Boston: Little, Brown, 1980.

4. "Applying the Death Penalty." *New York Times,* Letters to the Editor, Ernest van Den Haag, November 18, 1994. See, for example, "Six Lashes in Singapore." *Newsweek,* March 14, 1994: 29.

5. Steven Best, "Foucault, Postmodernism, and Social Theory." In David R. Dickens and Andrea Fontana, eds., *Postmodernism and Social Inquiry.* New York: Guilford, 1994: 28.

6. Michel Foucault, *Discipline and Punish.* Trans. A. M. Sheridan. New York: Pantheon, 1977.

7. Michel Foucault, "After word: The Subject of Power." In Hubert L. Dreyfus and Paul Rabinow, eds., *Michel Foucault: Beyond Structuralism and Hermeneutics.* Berkeley: University of California Press, 1983: 209.

8. For a summary of the U.S. experience with institutional social control during the pre- and postcolonial periods, see Rothman, 1971; 1980.

9. Lawrence Friedman, *A History of American Law.* New York: Simon and Schuster, 1973: 250.

10. I wrote about these developments in a previous book entitled *Castles of Our Conscience: Social Control and the American State, 1800–1985.* I would like to reiterate some of this history here, since I think it crucial to our understanding of our present-day situation.

11. Orlando Lewis, *The Development of American Prisons and Prison Customs, 1776–1845.* Albany: Prison Association of New York, 1922 [1967]: 18. Staples, 1991: 19–25.

12. Thomas Dumm, *Democracy and Punishment: Disciplinary Origins of the United States.* Madison: University of Wisconsin Press, 1987: 120.

13. "At Work, a Different Test for Drugs." *New York Times,* January 21, 1996: F11.

14. Robert M. Emerson and Sheldon M. Messinger, "The Micro-Politics of Trouble." *Social Problems* 25, 1977: 121–34.

15. Jeremy Bentham, "Preface." In Miran Bozovic, ed., *The Panopticon Writings.* London: Verso, 1995: 32.

16. Foucault, 1979: 211.

17. Ibid., 1979: 297.

18. Dreyfus and Rabinow, 1983: xxvi.

19. Foucault, 1979: 209.

20. Donald Lowe, *The Body in Late Capitalism USA.* Durham, N.C.: Duke University Press, 1995: 20.

21. Vaclav Havel, "The New Measure of Man." *New York Times,* July 8; 1994: D29.

22. Meyerowitz, cited in Lili Berko, "Surveying the Surveilled: Video, Space, and Subjectivity." *Quarterly Review of Film and Video,* 14, 1992: 61–91.
23. Norman K. Denzin, *Images of Postmodern Society: Social Theory and Contemporary Cinema.* London: Sage, 1991: viii.
24. "Heroin Ads Are Needle-Sharp." *Lawrence Journal-World,* June 18, 1996: 4A.
25. Keith Humphreys and Julian Rappaport, "From the Community Mental Health Movement to the War on Drugs: A Study in the Definitions of Social Problems." *American Psychologist* 48, 1993: 896.
26. According to Humphreys and Rappaport (1993: 895) budget authority for federal spending on interdiction, law enforcement, treatment, and prevention of drug abuse rose 679 percent during the decade 1981–91. In 1988 the majority of people arrested America's twenty-two largest cities were classified as "cocaine users."
27. "Get tough" suddenly meant "Go broke!" according to Ronald Corbett and Gary T. Marx in "Critique: No Soul in the New Machine: Technofallacies in the Electronic Monitoring Movement." *Justice Quarterly* 8, September, 1991:403. By 1987, thirty-seven states were under court-ordered mandate to end prison overcrowding, claims Joan Petersilia in *Expanding Options for Criminal Sentencing.* Santa Monica, Calif.: RAND, 1987.
28. David Altheide, "Gonzo Justice." *Symbolic Interaction* 15, 1993: 69–86. See also his "Electronic Media and State Control: The Case of Abscam." *Sociological Quarterly* 34, 1993: 53–69; and *Media Power.* Newbury Park, Calif.: Sage, 1985.
29. Stanley Cohen anticipated some of these developments in his important works *Visions of Social Control: Crime, Punishment and Classification.* Cambridge, U.K.: Polity Press; and "The Punitive City: Notes on the Dispersal of Social Control." *Contemporary Crisis* 3, 1979: 339–63.
30. "Idle Hands within the Devil's Own Playground." *New York Times,* July 16, 1995: E3.
31. Mike Davis, *City of Quartz.* London: Verso, 1990.

3

The Gaze and Its Compulsions

Disneyland is presented as imaginary in order to make us believe that the rest is real, when in fact all of Los Angeles and the America surrounding it are no longer real, but of the order of hyperreal and of simulation.
—Jean Baudrillard, *Simulations*[1]

Court TV: Watching the Real Life Drama of Justice . . . Just the reality of real reality television.
—Advertisement in the *New York Times*

Steve L., a convicted sex offender who lives in Tampa, Florida, returned home from work one day at 3 P.M., as required by his probation. At 4:09 he left his house for 17 minutes. The signal from the small radio transmitter attached to his ankle could no longer reach a monitoring box in the kitchen. Twenty miles away, a Florida Department of Corrections computer checked his work and treatment schedule, found that his brief absence was unauthorized, and sent an alarm to an office printer. The computer then automatically telephoned his probation officer.[2]

Much like Disneyland, Steve L.'s experience of "doing time at home" is a patchwork of preceding orders and futuristic possibilities. It is a near make-believe, virtual world where all values (order, authority, justice, discipline, freedom, consumption, work, self-help, etc.) are celebrated, simulated, and presented. It is a bit of what French social theorist Jean Baudrillard calls the *hyperreal*. How so? Hyperreality exists in a postmodern culture when there are no longer any "real," stable reference points. For example, while this kind of "electronic monitoring" is judged by its proponents to simulate the confinement experience of the prison, in practice, this popular new disciplinary technique bears little relation to *any* reality. We are told that offenders are "free" to participate in everyday life, yet their movements are highly regulated, the random gaze creating anxiety and, yes, obedience and docility.[3] Is this *real* freedom or a simulation? Steve L. is permitted to live at home, but is it "home," or is it "prison"? Is he a "convict" or a "client"? Is

41

his home "private" space or a simulation of the private that can come under the scrutiny of public authorities? These dichotomies no longer make any sense. If it *is,* and at the same time *is not,* "home," "prison," "private," or "freedom," then what is it?

These tangled notions are evident when officials discuss just what "house arrest" means. One advocate calls the concept a "winner" because it enables a person to maintain "the semblance of a normal life—even hold a job" (in other words, a simulated "normal" life). Another is critical, since agencies often fail to provide clients with "the kind of counseling they need to re-enter society." But aren't they already in society? Apparently not, according to the Superior Court of Arizona. The court ruled that a person under house arrest may be prosecuted for "escape" for unauthorized leaves, just as a prisoner may be prosecuted for breaking out of prison.[4] So then, "house arrest," once an odd-sounding contradiction in terms, has become part of the discourse and practice of justice officials who have normalized this simulation as accepted public policy. A client's home is characterized by some in this new discourse as simply another "correctional setting." It becomes, then, a "virtual" prison.

Within this hyperreality of house arrest, clients are rendered docile not through isolation and transformation of their "souls" during their *segregation* from society but rather through the surveillance of their bodies during *integration* into everyday postmodern life. During the industrial age of the nineteenth century, the "prison" (i.e., social segregation) and punishment were premised on the denial of "freedom" (i.e., social integration) and on the production of "useful" bodies trained to labor. Yet the social, cultural, and economic conditions of late capitalism shatter this theorem. Today, "useful" bodies are primarily consuming ones, and everyday life is marked by our growing dependency on the commodities that signal our desired lifestyles. Therefore, if formal, coercive social control is increasingly tied to social integration rather than to segregation, then "freedom" becomes simply that which can create, like the anklet device, the simulation of freedom.

SPIDERMAN MEETS ROBO COP

The brainchild of a New Mexico judge (who, it is said, was inspired—in a wonderful postmodern twist—by the use of a similar device in a 1979 Spiderman comic book), *electronically monitored home confinement,* or *EMHC,* programs, now tether more than thirty thousand individuals in nearly every state to central monitoring systems installed by community corrections officials. "It's just a given that business is going to grow," says one stock analyst speaking of the corporations that produce the devices.

"These are the companies working to solve a social problem of the 90s. . . . They are going to help develop the industry and . . . the state-of-the-art equipment that is going to be necessary."

This disciplinary technology has much in common with the past. Like Bentham's Panopticon, the anklet device permits near-constant surveillance of movement. With most systems, individuals cannot stray more then 150 feet or so from the monitoring box without triggering a violation. Random checks, day or night, bring the discretionary and one-dimensional gaze of authorities onto the clients; they never know when they may be called. One news article about these devices states that, "while confinement by monitor does not include bars, correction officials say the psychological loss of freedom should not be discounted." In order to "sharpen a convict's sense of confinement," officials often visit homes or workplaces unannounced, "even reciting the prisoner's every move the previous day" to make it clear to the client that he or she is being monitored. Speaking in perfect Panopticonese, one probation officer stated, "We want them to know we're watching even when they don't know we're watching." "In a way, monitors are better then prison 'cause you're still at home and all," states a Floridian spending two years with the device for an assault conviction. "But you got to ask someone permission to do everything, and I mean everything, man. You can't go nowhere without them knowing about it. And that way prison might be better 'cause you get it over with."[5] One system uses a monitoring video camera, instead of the pager-size anklet device. The Visitel camera is described by its manufacturer's agent this way: "The system is unique because there is a human connection that will talk with the offender. That person will ask the offender to smile, or turn his head, wave at the camera, or something like that to make sure it is the offender."[6] Indeed, this is the contemporary equivalent of the prisoner standing before the inspector's lodge.

But the ultimate application of this panoptic mechanism requires no agent at all. With this particular system, verifications are completed by the computer itself, programmed to dial at random times. "Hello," says the voice simulator, "This is a Community Control officer calling to verify that the person under our custody is at home. I will pause 10 seconds for the person to come to the phone." The prisoner is then told to state his or her name and the time of day. The system stores voice patterns in order to verify an offender's identity. The prisoner then puts the electronic anklet into a device which sends an electronic signal to the computer.[7] Whether triggering a spatial violation or offering one's voice to the machine, such decentralized control encourages "participatory monitoring" whereby those being watched become active "partners" in their own surveillance.[8]

Yet while Bentham's Panopticon was an archetype of modern discipline—and the anklet device a logical extension of it—this new technique is, at the same time, quintessentially *post*modern in design and implementation. The cybernetic life-world and video technology of contemporary society permit a new partitioning—a new "grid" of power—that extends into the everyday, in and through the gaze of community corrections. This new grid comes about because the anklet device no longer requires the boundaries or the division of space through the architecture of a building. Indeed, this exercise of power can operate more freely, down to the trivial extremities, the remotest corners, of everyday life, rather then be confined, like the offenders themselves, within walls of the modern asylum. Disciplinary power, then, has been deinstitutionalized and decentralized. Unlike the somewhat primitive panoptic tower that could practically view only a limited number of cells, the cybernetic machine is capable of creating an infinite number of confinements, as Foucault put it, "like so many cages, so many small theaters, in which each actor is alone, perfectly individualized and constantly visible."[9] With this technological marvel, we no longer have to worry about the cost of prison construction and administration. We now have in our grasp an inexhaustible supply of inexpensive, disciplinary "space."

The modern, nineteenth-century asylum once stood as a grand monument of state power displayed for all to see. The anklet device adheres to new principles of postmodern disciplinary power. Rather than a grand public display, it is nearly invisible to all, save the offender, yet it functions with great economy, constantly and efficiently.[10] It replaces the heaviness of the fortress with the simple, economic geometry of the semiconductor. As Foucault claimed, "The panoptic schema makes an apparatus of power more intense: it assures its economy (in material, in personnel, in time); it assures efficacy by its preventive character, its continuous functioning and its automatic mechanisms." Compared with the cost of building prison beds and the expense of confinement (more than $20,000 per inmate per year), EMHC systems require a small initial investment, few personnel to administer, and cost about $6.50 a day per person to operate. And rather than subject the body to a regimented system of institutional discipline and control, with EMHC the disciplinary technology is located on the body itself. As one inmate at a midwestern state penitentiary told me, "It's like carrying the state around on your ankle. I'd rather do my time in here and have them leave me alone."

First used on so-called nonviolent, felony offenders who were on parole from prison, the anklet devices are beginning to proliferate. For example, in my area, the devices are primarily used on juvenile offenders, some as young as 12, and on others who have been charged but have never been convicted of a crime. Interestingly, the central monitoring office of the computer company that is contracted for the service is located somewhere in Texas, about a thousand miles away. Presently, the systems in use cannot track a client who strays outside the range on the monitor. Yet I was told by one justice official that the next generation of devices will indeed be able to report the whereabouts of clients at all times, permitting police to quickly apprehend violators.

A COMMUNITY *OF* CORRECTIONS?

With the extended reach of such "community"-based programs, the authority to judge individuals goes far beyond the walls of the prison that may have formally held them or any notion of a modest punishment for an offense committed. Now the gaze and surveillance of authorities can go straight into an individual's home, school, or work place and can evaluate, assess, and enforce, if necessary, the person's "progress" on the road to becoming an idealized citizen. This kind of power is, indeed, capillary, circulating freely, far below the central administration of the state to the tiniest corners of society, and exercised by low-level criminal justice bureaucrats and technicians armed with a new discourse of accountability and what are referred to by practitioners as "case-management devices."

Anyone who thinks that "doing time at home" is "easy time" knows little about these contemporary programs. One official told me that being sentenced to a community corrections programs was, in many ways, much "harder time" than sitting in a jail cell. For example, consider the *intensive supervision programs (ISP)* now operating in many communities throughout the country. These are designed for adult, nonviolent felons so that they may, according to one report, "remain in the community while becoming responsible, accountable, and self-supporting." One ISP requires a minimum of four contacts per week between a "client" and an intensive supervision officer (ISO) during the first year in the program. During this time, the ISO is charged with directing daily job searches, verification of employment through the provision of "pay stubs," initiating at least one monthly meeting with employers or training/education providers (not including unannounced visits), coordinating community service work (40 hours per week for those unemployed; 5 hours for those employed), collecting court-ordered restitution, initiating client curfews (enforced by means of electronic monitoring if deemed necessary), running weekly computerized record checks, and performing random drug and alcohol tests on all participants. After successfully completing the first eight months in the program with no "major violations," an offender may progress to less-intensive surveillance "at the discretion of the ISO."[11]

I spent some time talking with directors and intensive supervision staff of several community corrections programs, and I took a monitoring tour with one agency's "Surveillance Officer" (his official title). "Pete," a twenty-year veteran of law enforcement and military policing, is responsible for checking up on program "clients" (both juveniles and adults) on weekends and evenings. He does so by driving around the county, stopping in on clients at random times, making sure they are at home as scheduled, generally checking up on them, and performing drug and alcohol tests. (I discuss these techniques in more detail in Chapter 4.) Pete records his findings on a clipboard, jotting down the results of the tests as well as noting that the client was "watching TV" or had a "friend visiting," and the like. Sometimes he would "double back" on a client, 15 or 20 minutes after his first visit, in order to "keep 'em honest."

From the eyes of an "outsider" like myself, Pete's ritualized visits to a client's home—sometimes as late as 11:30 P.M.—had an absurd and unnerving quality. I kept trying to imagine what it would be like to have someone come knocking on my door this late at night for what amounts to a very personal inspection. Indeed, it seemed clear to me that, while not exactly a prison, an offender's home was transformed into a "correctional setting" in terms of the loss of privacy and the institutionlike rituals the occurred with Pete's arrival. Despite this, every client I observed greeted Pete in a friendly manner as he walked—without hesitation or invitation—into their homes. It was obvious that these people "knew the drill" of Pete's visits, just as they knew the rituals of alcohol and drug testing. His showing up seemed as "normal" to them as the arrival of the mail carrier. I was struck by how much Pete knew about their lives—not only the typical things that were likely to be in their files but also the numerous details about their friends, their habits, their likes and dislikes, their medical and family histories, who among them were likely to be the "success stories" and who were likely to "screw up." And "screw up" they do. One measure of the difficulty of the program is, according to its director, the fact that 50 percent of adult clients fail to complete their "contract" with the court (this appears to be typical of other programs throughout the country). Given what he called the "intrusive" nature of the surveillance program—"We're out there every night, weekends and holidays"—it seems it would be difficult not to "screw up."

Moreover, as one program director told me, once such programs are put in place, judges begin to assign what he considered to be "inappropriate" offenders to the program, such as "low-risk" misdemeanants, juveniles waiting for hearings, adults convicted of nonaggravated sex offenses, and the like. Previously, these people would have been released or would have done short jail time, had the program not been available.

But once people are under the constant gaze of authorities, other infractions may be uncovered; files get thicker, and the minor offender
becomes the known "drug user" or the "kid with serious problems."
These people, of course, are deserving of even more surveillance, and so
it goes. This process has the effect of "widening the net" of the justice system and drawing in people who might not otherwise have been there.
Interestingly, after being told that an increasing number of "sex offenders" was being assigned to one program, I asked officials why someone
convicted of sex crimes should be tested regularly for alcohol (a legal
substance) and drug use. No one could give me a reasonable answer, saying only that it was "part of the program." Once established, then, programs like intensive supervision become general disciplinary tools that
are used to let certain individuals "know we're watching even when they
don't know we're watching" whether that form of surveillance is "appropriate" for them or not.

Finally, Pete told me, with little thought or question, that the ISP was
"obviously better than putting them away." He repeatedly stressed the
"productive" and "self-training and discipline" capacities of the community corrections scheme throughout our conversations. When I asked
him, for example, what he thought his clients felt about wearing an electronic anklet device, he said, "They appreciate that it's an option." He
went on to relate stories about clients who themselves had requested to
be in the program, in order to "clean up" from drugs or to "stop running
with the wrong crowd."

"INTERVENTION OPPORTUNITIES"

As I suggested in Chapter 2, I see these new community-based forms of
surveillance as an extension of the disciplinary power first deployed in
closed institutions. Once lodged in the community, however, they begin
to reach out, to invest, colonize, and link up with other organizations and
practices, thereby creating a network of social control. This is clear when
we see the blurring distinctions among the legal, justice, and social welfare functions of these programs. During one of my rounds with Pete the
surveillance officer, for example, he received a cellular phone call from a
police dispatcher (he is not a law enforcement officer) who asked him
questions about, and later had him call, one of his clients concerning a
domestic dispute at her house. Another community corrections program
I looked at has, in addition to the ISP, nearly a dozen other programs that
it administers (and will even contract out to neighboring counties)
including domestic violence intervention, rape crisis, victim-witness
assistance, homes for children "at risk," educational services for clients,

and the *family training program,* or *FTP.* The stated goal of the FTP component is to prevent the incarceration of the adult offender by tracking not only the offender but family members as well. The program involves an in-home style of intervention. Yet, despite the best intentions of its practitioners, it is a model that, I argue, significantly facilitates and enhances the exercise of disciplinary power. With this view in mind, consider how proponents characterize their activities. A report from the community corrections agency describes the FTP this way:

> By improving the stability of the offender and his/her family, there is a much higher likelihood that the offender will be productive and avoid additional criminal behavior that would result in incarceration. This goal is obtained by physically working in the home and teaching new parenting skills and child management skills to parents who have exhibited weaknesses in these areas. . . . This is accomplished by a therapist of the Family Training Program going into the home and providing intense therapy within the home setting. In addition to scheduled appointments, the therapist will make intermittent unannounced visits in order to gain a more realistic view of the families interaction and the use of the new skills.[12]

In fact, the "home-based" and "family preservation" models have become the most popular forms of "service delivery" throughout what one could call the burgeoning penal/health/welfare complex. For example, others see the supposedly therapeutic agendas of community mental health programs this way:

> Practitioners constantly seek innovative ways to improve service delivery to high-risk children and families who are isolated and unlikely to seek help at an agency. Home-based practice is rapidly becoming an alternative to practice in office settings [providing for] . . . enhanced assessment and intervention opportunities. . . .[13]

> Home visits [that] allow therapists . . . direct observation of a family in the natural environment of their home can bring into focus more quickly the significant dynamics in the family and can help guide treatment. Therapy moved into the home setting occurs in a heightened reality context that includes the possible participant-observer role of the therapist, more active involvement of family members, and the opportunity

for immediate analysis of family members' actual behavior.[14]

These kinds of home-based models, then, provide the means by which case workers, therapists, and others extend the gaze of disciplinary power into the daily lives of clients. As "experts," they are charged with making normalizing judgments not only about their clients but also about their entire families. (Are they "functional" or "dysfunctional"? Are they "multiproblem"? Do they have "borderline" personalities? Are they "at-risk"? Do they have the right "parenting skills"? Do they use drugs? Do the kids go to school? Etc.) And even if, as individuals, these well-intended professionals do not want to become the "eyes of the law," they are often compelled, *by law*, to report any illegal behavior they observe to the appropriate authorities. Or take the situation where social welfare officials are trying to decide whether a child should be "reintegrated" back into a home after the family has been deemed "unfit." "This is when the team has to decide to let go," according to one social worker I talked to. (The "team" is made up of the core members of what is called a "wrap-around" treatment model that brings in welfare case workers, individual and family therapists, agency lawyers, and a host of others professionals.) In this case, the previously "unfit" family must meet the standard of the more idealized, "functional" foster family the child may be living with. The possibility of "letting go" creates considerable anxiety on the part of the worker because, "It's hard to extract the kid out of this great home and put him back in with borderlines." While most of us might be able to identify cases of, say, physical abuse, one has to wonder what criteria are used to determine who is "borderline" and who is not. Just where is the line between a "functional" versus an "unfit" family? Who gets to decide what "parenting skills" are appropriate, while other skills are not? The fact is, this is not a science but a series of socially constructed judgments. I wonder how many American families could survive the assessment and be labeled a "great home" if our behaviors were observed, scrutinized, and clinically diagnosed.

THE JUSTICE "FISHBOWL"

With community policing and corrections, neighborhood detention centers, offenders under arrest in their own homes, and the proliferation of in-home social welfare models, we see then the process whereby disciplinary power leaches into everyday life. To reiterate Foucault, it is where the "massive, compact disciplines—the jail, the prison, the poorhouse, and the mental hospital—are broken down into flexible methods of control, which may be transferred and adapted." The next logical step in "decentralizing" the penal/heath/welfare complex is to bring courts to the local level as well. One model—simply riddled with postmodern themes—that is being heralded as a prototype court of the future was opened recently in New York City's Times Square district. Supported and actually financed by private developers who have spent billions "rehabing" the seedy district into a tourist mecca, this specialized "boutique" court deals only with street hustlers, graffiti artists, prostitutes, and shoplifters who traditionally had been "kicked" by uptown courts too busy with felony cases. The court will process more than fifteen thousand of these so-called quality-of-life offenders this year. It is characterized as a "computer-driven laboratory," a "fishbowl" that puts a "judge under the same roof as city health workers, drug counselors, schoolteachers and nontraditional community service outlets."

A Digital Equipment Corporation computer is at the center of the management information system. It acts, according to one writer who observed the court,

> as the receptor for an elaborate system of remote feeds which, when combined, create the equivalent of a three-inch court file that can be accessed from a single screen. The process usually begins with a beat cop issuing a complaint to an offender, complete with a date for him or her to appear in court. Copies of the complaints are sent to the Manhattan DA's office, which in turn faxes them to the court.
>
> When the defendant arrives in the new courthouse, his presence is noted on large screens that hang in the entrance way like airport flight monitors, displaying the names of all those scheduled to appear that day. . . . In addition, a dozen monitors jam the interior well of the courtroom. . . . If all has worked, the faxed complaint from the DA's office has been scanned into the computer and can be pulled up from any of those monitors. Ditto the defendant's rap sheet, which gets fed into the database by an online hookup with the state's Division of Criminal Justice.
>
> Before long, an interviewer approaches the defendant with a laundry list of queries: Does he or she have a drug habit, a home, a job? Each answer is typed into a laptop computer and downloaded into the DEC machine. . . . By now thousands of bits of information about a single defendant are swimming around the electronic file folder.

As the man who designed the court says, "We know very little about the 100,000 people who come through this system. In three years, we're going to know a whole lot more."[15]

THE TRANSPARENT SOCIETY

If postmodern culture is one characterized by an implosion of previously accepted boundaries, we see, as well, the disintegration of the barriers that once offered us some form of sanctuary. "Such a society," according to Ronald Corbett and Gary Marx, "is transparent and porous. Information leakage is rampant. Barriers and boundaries—distance, darkness, time, walls, windows, and even skin, which have been fundamental to our conceptions of privacy, liberty and individuality—give way."[16] This condition has been brought about by the emergence of what Marx calls the "new surveillance": an optical revolution engendered by a dizzying array of digitized, computer/video/telecommunication devices that have made watching and monitoring deftly penetrating yet seamless and hidden. In our post–Cold War world, certain government agencies and former defense contractors have found a lucrative market in the "security" business. With developments in night-vision technology, auditory devices, telecommunications monitoring, and the like, the state, as well as private organizations and individuals, has an arsenal of surveillance gadgets at its disposal. In the next few sections I will introduce you to some of them.

The video camera, for example, has fundamentally altered the nature of policing as well as the entire U.S. justice system. Videocams, mounted on the dashboards of patrol cars, are rapidly becoming a central feature in the daily lives of the police and those they encounter. Activated automatically whenever an officer turns on the car's flashing lights, the devices are a "real asset to everyone involved," according to one law enforcement official. "Tapes can be played in court," states a news article, "to give jurors an unadulterated account of the crime. Instead of hearing disputed testimony about a drunk driver's impaired driving, for instance, jurors could see the car weaving. The footage also serves for unimpeachable evidence of evaluating deputies. Video of officer's conduct—correct or incorrect—could be used in training."[17]

Indeed. On the evening of March 3, 1991, four Los Angeles police officers were secretly videotaped beating unarmed motorist Rodney King. The widespread dissemination of these images created a media spectacle that was turned against the police department and the city. So, in order to bring more visibility to this shadowed space, law enforcement officials began immediately to experiment with installing video cameras in police cars. The same device used to expose this atrocity would now "protect" both the officers and their suspects. "I think they have the ability to bring credibility back to law enforcement," states one official about the use of such cameras. "When you're on TV, you don't do bad things. The officer acts his best and the actions are documented." The camera does not discriminate; its gaze is both controlling and productive as it disciplines the conduct of both suspects and police. It provides then an elegant solution to the question: "Who is guarding the guards?" demonstrating the role of "hierarchical observation" as each individual carries out the act of watching others while he or she is also being watched. The visual technology not only empowers the calculated gaze and watches and renders the suspect docile but, as Foucault put it, also "constantly supervises the very individuals who are entrusted with the task of supervising."

Like other technologies, videocams are becoming so inexpensive and small they can be used almost anywhere. A "badge-size" camera or "personal video surveillance system" was introduced recently by Semco Company of Carlsbad, California, that sends the image back to the recording unit in the police car. The company says that the device is particularly useful in recording combative suspects and in dealing with false-arrest lawsuits. Video technology is currently used in documenting interrogations and confessions, undercover investigations, lineups, crime scenes and their reenactment, the testimony of victims and witnesses and the physical condition of suspects during booking, lockups, and on and on. One interesting use of the videocam has been to link judges and defendants during preliminary hearings and other procedural steps in the justice system. Rather than take the time and incur the cost of transporting numerous offenders to the courthouse from correctional facilities, the participants merely view each other on a monitor—constituting a sort of efficient "virtual habeas corpus," if you will. Just imagine yourself as a defendant, watching your own preliminary hearing on a video screen while the television in the game room blares reruns of a gritty "reality" justice show or has live coverage of today's "trial of the century." The process of "justice" becomes yet another videoscape in the day-to-day world of the postmodern.

Like the videocams in the police cars, these cameras contribute plenty of grist for the "real" cop and justice shows and other media spectacles. In fact, the justice system has felt intense pressure from the media to gain direct access to this world. Recently, after several years of resistance, New York City permitted the cable channel Court TV to begin filming a series called *The System* in and around the 101st Precinct in Far Rockaway. Videocam operators ride along with police, film arrests and bookings, and follow defendants through trial "like a nonfiction version of the NBC drama 'Law and Order,'" according to one news article. But wait: Isn't *Law and Order* supposed to be a "reality" drama based on the "true" stories of the justice system? So is the filming of *The System* a case of life imitating art that, itself, was supposed to be imitating life? An official from the police commissioner's office stated that the filming will "help to tell a less-sensational story about the lives of officers and the true nature of police work." It may also provide a way of keeping his eye on his officers in a department plagued by allegations of police corruption and illegal behavior.[18]

In Contra Costa, California, the television is used in another way. Here, a county supervisor, the district attorney, and about a dozen custodial parents have gotten together to produce a pubic-access show they call *Costra County's Deadbeat Parents*. The show, playing on eleven cable systems in the area, is modeled after the national series *America's Most Wanted* and shows a picture of the malfeasant parent while an announcer narrates the person's height, weight, race, last known occupation, and number of minor children. Each month the show includes a new crop of "deadbeats" from the county's roster. If viewers identify one of the parents, they are asked to call the district attorney's office: "We hope you'll wake up and tap him of the shoulder and say, 'Hey pal. I'm tired of paying *my* taxes to support *your* kids.'"[19]

"POWER-SEEING"

Although video technology and its gaze have become commonplace in the justice system, they appear downright primitive when compared with what may be on the horizon. For example, one headline reads, "New Scanners May Redefine Strip Search," and the article describes researchers at a federally financed laboratory who have developed a "holographic radar scanner" that can peer through clothing in order to see hidden objects. There are two prototypes: one is a walk-in booth that scans the entire body, while the other is a handheld device that is aimed at specific body parts.[20] Meanwhile, the FBI is pushing for the widespread adoption of the NCIC 2000 computer system that is being installed in some police cars. This system allows police not only to confirm outstanding arrest warrants but also to store and transmit photographic images and fingerprints for identification and matching.[21] Once these sources of identification are digitized, widespread and instant dissemination is possible. In Kansas, the legislature recently adopted a computerized system for placing ID pictures on driver's licenses, providing police with convenient and essentially open access to this information. A lobbyist for several state law enforcement associations said the change to the digitized system would "promote effective criminal investigations."[22]

State troopers who set up random safety inspections on interstate highways are being issued a new high-tech tool called an "Ion-Scanner." These portable devices, passed over the logbooks of long-haul truck drivers, are capable of identifying drug residue. A positive reading justifies "probable cause" for searching the vehicle.[23] And in the self-declared "war" against marijuana growers in the Pacific Northwest, National Guard units are already using military technology such as night-vision goggles to flush out growers. Aided by drug enforcement experts from the Pentagon, the National Guard has turned to using thermal imaging devices to sense the heat seeping from growing lamps in homes, attics, and barns.[24]

Yet this may be only the beginning of the uses of military technology for domestic "crime fighting" and the like. Lessons are being learned from so-called postmodern wars like the conflict in the former Yugoslavia. Here nation-states are replaced by fragmented militias where the lack of a central authority makes the conflict seemingly intractable. Live images of death and suffering are distributed worldwide and "sap whatever will or ability there may be to prosecute a devastating military campaign."[25] The role of groups like the United Nations becomes primarily one of "peacekeeping," and this necessitates intense "intelligence-gathering" and surveillance capabilities to monitor the parties involved. In Bosnia, for example, the U.S. military command post is called "Battlestar." Here is how one reporter described the installation:

> Basically, you have tiers set up, and each department and each unit has its representative there sitting in front of a laptop, and they're all facing what's essentially a large console that has TV sets and computer monitors and a bridge, basically, where the generals sit. *And, I mean, it's just as wired as can be. They can see virtually anything they want to see.* . . . And, they have devices that allow them to view live photos, say, from Apache helicopters that are out in the field. *It's probably the most surveilled landscape in the history of the world.* . . .
>
> There is a system called *"power-seeing,"* and what it allows is them to take satellite photographs that already exist and put them over maps and create, basically, 3-D layouts so that, in fact, before anybody actually went into Bosnia, people down to the company command level had actually practiced with power-seeing flying through the route they were going to take, and see things down to the scale of buildings and intersections and railroads. And, it's like a video game. You have a joy-stick and you can kind of weave your way through. . . .

> We went out on a night patrol, and a lot of people
> have global positioning satellite readers. So, they know
> exactly where they are. And, everybody, virtually, has
> one kind of night-vision goggle. And, *it's a camera* [as
> well] and you have two eye pieces. In the eye pieces you
> see kind of a green and white representation of the
> landscape. (Emphasis mine)[26]

I would not be surprised to find "power-seeing" technology being deployed in the coming years by police departments in South Central Los Angels, Detroit, or Philadelphia.

With considerable pressure from the Clinton administration and the FBI, the Senate voted unanimously to support the so-called wiretap bill of 1994. This bill forces phone companies to make their emerging digital networks accessible to law enforcement agencies. Currently, these agencies need a court order to "tap" a conventional copper-wire phone line. With the new digital networks, the FBI wants to be able to listen in on as many as 1 percent of all phone calls made in what is referred to as a "high-crime" geographical area. This could mean that law enforcement agencies could be monitoring hundreds, perhaps thousands of calls, whether or not there was any probable cause for listening in. With access to the network software, monitoring someone's phone (or any other communication device connected to the network, such as a computer) will be quite simple. No need to climb telephone poles; no clicking and cracking on the line; in an age of fiber optics, cellular grids, satellite uplinks, and "the Net," the word *wiretap* is a quaint reminder of a bygone era.[27]

While law enforcement personnel rave about the next generation of weapons in their war on crime, others folks contend that the technology is subject to abuse and is prone to error, making many of the new devices a threat to our constitutional rights. For example, several lawsuits have been filed against the use of patrol-car computer systems. When police arrested a man on U.S. Route 1 in New Jersey in early 1995, it was not because they observed him doing anything illegal. Rather, the officers simply decided to run his vehicle's license plate through their the patrol-car computer. It told them that he had a suspended license. But in a case filed with the state courts, the man contends that the police singled him out arbitrarily—without reasonable suspicion or probable cause—and that the resulting computer search of his record was illegal. Others have sued because they were arrested for outstanding warrants that had in fact been cleared but were never deleted by a clerk. A representative from one privacy group stated: "They [the police] should not be able to go out willy-nilly to investigate everyone on a whim or a hunch. I mean the British in 1776 were saying, 'We're trying to investigate illegal smuggling, and you only have to worry about it if you're guilty.' But they were investigating everyone's houses."[28]

Meanwhile, we are seeing the emergence of *intelligent transportation systems,* or "smart highways," that attempt to rationally regulate traffic flows, alert drivers to accident scenes and other tie-ups, and automatically collect tolls at access points. Some of these systems are already operating. In the Los Angeles area, video cameras mounted along freeways feed information to the central offices of the state's transportation department. In Florida, a system called E-pass on the Orlando–Orange County Expressway automatically deducts tolls from vehicles that have a transponder mounted under the front bumper. In Kansas, when a similar system was installed recently, highway authorities mailed out 12,000 transponders in the first week. Users marveled at the new system. "I just can't believe how convenient it is," one man stated. "The arm swings up and away we go, and wave to everyone else waiting in line."[29] Getting ahead of the line, however, comes at the price of a little less privacy. These systems are capable of generating a data set of the time, date, and location of each toll collected. Currently, the U.S. Department of Transportation is working on a plan to have a national standard for the devices so that they would work on roads across the country. The "dark side" of the plan, as pointed out by Simson Garfinkel, writing in the *New York Times,* is that "it offers unprecedented opportunities to monitor the movements of drivers. It would create a bank of personal information that the government and private industry might have difficultly resisting."[30] He cites the case of auto insurance companies, for example, that might want to use the data to assess their relative risk of insuring someone based on the person's driving habits.

A similar system is being proposed by the California Air Resources Board, the state's air-quality management and regulatory agency. A new law requires new cars, after 1996, to be equipped with a computer that monitors and informs the owner of possible emissions malfunctions. But in order to make sure that the clean air standard is maintained, the board wants those computers to be fitted with a transponder that could be "read" by a technician during biannual inspections. In addition, the board sees the devices as being capable of routinely monitoring compliance by installing roadside receivers that would quickly let authorities know if the vehicle was in violation. Identification of the owner from the vehicle plate number means that an inspection notice—or ticket—might soon arrive in the mail.[31] Of course, similar lessons were learned from the use of automatic cameras that have been in employed for some years in the United States and Europe, whereby speeding motorists trigger a camera that takes a picture of their license plates and automatically issues them a citation.

These examples highlight another postmodern paradox: that the gaze is increasingly secured through the very products and services (such as the automobile) that we are seduced into consuming. Portable phones are easily listened in on, and inexpensive video technology ensures that cameras and their tapes abound; meanwhile, emerging computer networks make our activities and correspondence easier to monitor. Is this what David Lyon has called "pleasurable" social control?[32] Moreover, Lili Berko argues that the proliferation of devices also increases the "pool of watchers" and fundamentally changes our role in the surveillance gaze. "In this way," she states, "the postmodern panopticon moves beyond Bentham's model . . . to a postmodern model, in which individuals enjoy the possibility of becoming the owners and operators of the personal and professional seeing machines. . . ."[33] Two recent examples will illustrate. First, the disappearance of a child in California turned the Internet's 20-million-plus worldwide users, 250 bulletin-board participants, and thousands of facsimile-machine owners into "watchers." One of the individuals involved suggested that the dissemination of the girl's image was "like a good virus: it proliferated." The case seems to have laid the groundwork for "lightning fast searchers in the future. At some point, ordinary citizens linked by nothing but goodwill and a keyboard will be able to check nation-wide bulletin boards devoted to cases of missing children."[34] In the second case, the *New York Times* headline read: "Thousands of Eyes for State Police"; "Florida asks cell phone users for help on the highways." "A lot of people want to get involved," said one officer, "and this is a good way to do it." Yet even the police see the possibility that *too much* surveillance might not be very practical. "We just don't have the resources to handle the calls if they call for every minor little thing."[35]

A CULTURE OF VOYEURS

Few of us stop to think about just how often, on any given day, we are being monitored or filmed by cameras. But it's not simply a kind of one-way, "Big Brother" surveillance that is going on. As a society, we have become obsessed with the gaze of the videocam, not only because we perceive that it brings us "security" but also because we are fascinated by the visual representation of ourselves. We are today, very much, a culture of voyeurs. This "playful" and "serious" fascination with the camera's eye results, I argue, in the normalization of the gaze in everyday life. As videocams are used around the house to capture our foibles and to make us all "stars" on *America's Funniest Home Videos*, they make us more and more comfortable with, and even drawn to, the idea of being preserved on tape. The proliferation of video means that we can all be "on film," just like our cherished cultural icons of television and the cinema. A state of "permanent visibility" looms over us as cameras and their tapes encroach into everyday life.

Today, the ubiquitous video "security" camera stares blankly at us in apartment buildings, department and convenience stores, gas stations, libraries, parking garages, automated banking outlets, buses, elevators, and the like. But as we are watched and monitored, we are also called to join in on the watching. Programs like *America's Most Wanted* call on the public to "join the force," as it were, and to provide information about criminals on the loose. Mimicking this style, a TV station in Kansas City, Missouri (no doubt like other local stations across the country), regularly runs "real" surveillance footage in it's popular "Crime Stoppers" segment, calling on the public to provide information about incidents. (When no videotape is available, some programs simply offer a "reenactment" of the crime with actors and props, dramatizing its menacing threat.) A favorite of the recent spate of tabloid news and entertainment television programs such as *Hard Copy*, for example, are segments like "Caught on Tape" that depict an array of behaviors or circumstances observed by the camera, including illegal activities that have been taped by law enforcement agencies. One recent show included tape—supposedly from infrared night cameras—of "bandits" crossing over the U.S. border from Mexico into El Paso, Texas. Finally, the Kansas City TV station mentioned earlier also has cameras set up around the "neighborhood" (in fact, a rather large metropolitan area involving several cities) to monitor the weather throughout its viewing area (and, you can bet, to catch any other story that happens to be played out in front of the camera's eye). "Let's just pop on over to the Plaza," chimes the effervescent weatherperson, "and see what's happening out there."

Our obsession with the gaze of the videocam leads to some amazing behavior. Take the two cases of teenagers—perhaps the first true video generation—who went about, seemingly illogically, *filming their own deviant activities*. In one instance, a group of kids drove around Los Angeles's San Fernando Valley and, over the course of several nights, made tapes of themselves smashing car windows with baseball bats and shooting bikers and pedestrians with an air rifle. In another case, a 16-year-old in Omaha had his friend videotape his premeditated assault on a younger student in the halls of their high school. Both tapes, of course, were then used as legal evidence against the adolescents. Like the Los Angeles incident, a version of the Omaha tape was played over and over again in the national media, the significance of the event taking on epic proportions. As one Associated Press story put it, "The attack in a high school lasted less than 30 seconds, but as a symbol of teen violence it will be around much longer."[36]

Evidence from the growing popularity of the World Wide Web, the Internet's multimedia component (combining text, sound, graphics, and video), is further testimony to the voyeuristic tendencies in the culture. A search of "home pages" devoted to "voyeurism" revealed a dozen or more involved in the distribution, exchange, and sale of erotic pictures and video taken of people without their knowledge. One site called "The Peep Hole" includes "hidden" camera footage from restrooms, hotels, clothing-store dressing rooms, and high school locker rooms as well as clips from the "eye in the sky" security cameras of gambling casinos, department stores, elevators, and the like. Other people prefer to turn the cameras on themselves and offer explicit "amateur" video available for anyone to view.

"The Web Voyeur" (rated in the top 5 percent of Web pages by Point Communications, Inc.) is a site designed for people to view, "in real time," various places around the world. Anyone with a computer and access to the Internet can "surf" through "live" images generated by cameras set up in more than a hundred settings including schools, bus stops, and even people's homes. According to the page's creator, more than 3,500 people a day "fritter away their precious free time looking at this page," where they can see "Outdoor Vistas . . . Indoor Surveillance . . . Personal Places . . . The Virtual Zoo . . . Simply Strange . . . Not Quite Live." The page includes such places as:

Aloha Tower, Honolulu, Hawaii

Hauptbahnof train/bus terminal/zoo, Berlin, Germany

Bermuda Biological Station for Research

Bus stop, Wilshire Boulevard, Beverly Hills, California (If you see a drug deal going down, report it to the Beverly Hills cops, not to me.)

Cambridge panorama, Cambridge, England (Nicely done! On the info page, you can zoom in on parts of the view or even call up Web servers in visible buildings, courtesy of Olivetti Research Labs.)

Cheyenne Mountain, Colorado Springs, Colorado (Keep an eye on this one when nuclear war breaks out.)

East Carolina University, School of Education parking lot, Greenville, North Carolina

The Hollywood sign, Hollywood, California

San Francisco Bay, San Francisco, California (Oh, baby, this is beautiful—at least until it gets dark! A view from the roof of the Fairmont Hotel, courtesy of KPIX-TV.)

Street corner (9th & Pearl), Boulder, Colorado (This is every bit as exciting as it sounds.)

Street corner (Hollywood & Vine), Hollywood, California (Up-to-the-minute view of Hollywood's most famous intersection; keep an eye out for guys kissing cops.)

Buckman Elementary School, Room 100, Portland, Oregon

SBT Accounting Systems, visitors' lobby, San Rafael, California

Adam Curry's office, New Jersey (Come on, admit it: Even this is better than MTV.)

Bull Creek Cam, Austin, Texas (Actually, it's the home/office of Mike Bryant, who allows us two camera views within his home.)

The list goes on and on. By linking video and computer technology, this home page hints at the possible creation of an enormous network of videocams, "jacked" into the Net, providing extraordinary voyeuristic, surveillance, and monitoring capabilities.

Interestingly, one of the most radical uses of a "network" of videocams for "security" purposes has occurred in Great Britain. In 1986 in the moderately sized market town of King's Lynn in Norfork, owners of an industrial park set up just three cameras in order to counteract a rash of burglaries. After two years, the problem "virtually disappeared" according to the owners. Local officials were so enamored with the cameras that they went on to install Great Britain's most sophisticated urban security system, known as *closed-circuit television,* or *CCTV.* Forty-five cameras monitor a community center, seventeen car parks, and the streets in both an industrial park and a housing complex. The cameras feed a central monitoring station that operates twenty-four hours a day, has twenty-two video screens, and provides a direct link to local police who permit the images to be sent to their station. The cameras can scan areas and zoom in on activity at the operator's will. On one U.S. television program about the use of the cameras in King's Lynn, the reporter asked an operator if he had ever used the cameras to "watch and follow pretty women or to get the plate number off their cars." He blushed and said "No," but when the reporter persisted, he admitted that he had in fact done this. The manufacturer of CCTV contends that, within five years, "Every town in Britain will have a similar system." Today, Great Britain leads the world in the use of public surveillance cameras. It appears that most people in King's Lynn have accepted the idea of being on camera. Some say it makes them feel "secure." And on one "productive" note, a local radio station relies on images from the cameras to tell people driving into town where they can find parking spaces.

Much like the nineteenth-century advocates of a more rational system of justice, the police in King's Lynn think that the cameras provide more efficient and more effective social control. They cite, for example, the case of children playing on their bikes in a car park when one decides to write graffiti on a wall. Alerted by the cameras, the police arrive, confront the juvenile, and make him clean up the wall. This way, the police claim, "the whole incident—crime, detection, and restoration—was over in less than five minutes, and dealt with informally, without the child having to be taken to the police station." Moreover, like the all-seeing, all-knowing "god" of the Panopticon, the mere presence of the camera's gaze appears to have the power to expedite "justice." Police say that the tapes from the system are rarely needed in court because "most people who are caught on tape confess as soon as they are told of the tape's existence, without even seeing it."[37]

Ironically, while the tapes may turn out to be "rarely needed" for the justice function they are supposed to serve, they are being gobbled up by the public as voyeuristic entertainment. Seeing a potential market for the tapes, one enterprising young man decided to purchase footage from insurance companies, security firms, and local governmental authorities. "Caught on Tape" and the sequel "Really Caught on Tape" contain snippets of things like a man being beaten during a store robbery, supposed drug dealers bashing each other with pipes, office workers having sex in a storeroom, and one woman (described on the tape as a "shoplifter") disrobing in a department store dressing room. The producer of the tapes claims that they were created as a form of protest against the surveillance cameras, but he admits they are making him some money. "We sold 60,000 in the first morning," he said, and they have ordered another 125,000 copies of the sequel. "When it comes down to video journalism—and that is what we claim to be—we're total hypocrites."[38]

Not to be outdone by the British, the city of Baltimore has been moving to a similar system. By the end of 1996, more than two hundred video cameras will be installed, monitoring nearly every street corner in the city's downtown district. The videotaping began near the popular Lexington Market, which is reported to have been "plagued by crime and loiterers" according to one news article.[39] The effort is being spearheaded and funded by a private group called the Downtown Partnership of Baltimore that brings together city and private funds to "promote downtown businesses." The cameras are mounted on traffic-signal posts and will be monitored 16 hours a day by police, who will be stationed in new, slightly oversized telephone-booth substations positioned throughout the area. According to Police Commissioner Thomas Frazier, the 96-hour-long tapes will be destroyed unless police or prosecutors decide that a crime may have been committed. The tapes, the commissioner assured the public, would never be handed over to any private investigators. Dismissing questions about the cameras' being an infringement on a citizen's constitutional rights, he claimed, "It's not an invasion of anybody's privacy. It's filming what you can already see."[40] Massachusetts officials have made similar claims about their plan to put videocams at traffic intersections to catch violators. "People say, 'Gee, this is Big Brother. This is 1984,'" said one legislator. "No, this is 1996."[41]

WE HEAR YOU

A growing number of retail stores in the United States are adding audio surveillance to complement their video monitors. Dunkin' Donuts stores, for example, were highlighted recently for the use of such listening technology. A security systems company representative in the state of Massachusetts claims that more than three hundred of the stores in that state have audio monitoring on the premises. A Dunkin' Donuts corporate spokesperson asserts that the systems are there to increase security and to keep employees "on their toes," not to listen in on customers. Yet the CEO of Louroe Electronics of Van Nuys, California, a manufacturer of the devices, claims that his system can pick up conversations as far as 30 feet away. "Unfortunately," he claims, "this is going to be the future until we get to the point of minimal crime in this country. Until then, store owners are going to have to have these devices to protect their employees and their customers."[42]

Far from the local donut shop, it is becoming increasingly common for lawyers to secretly tape-record conversations with clients, witnesses or the opposing counsel. Attorneys who use this tactic claim that they need the data as insurance against witnesses who might recant a story or fellow bar members who might welch on a deal. Yet some professional ethics committees have argued that the taping is clearly deceptive and thus unethical. One committee member has stated that the practice "discourages people from looking at lawyers as people who can be trusted and who are to some extent above the more shifty, shady proclivities of other professions" (apparently, not high enough above, for some). Last year, the New York County Lawyers' Association arrived at the extraordinary conclusion that such recording was not unethical as long as one party to the conversation—the person *doing* the taping—"consented" to it. Likewise, thirty-nine other states, including New York, allow taping under these conditions. Besides, proponents say, the technology has become so easy to use and the practice is so widespread that people should simply assume it is being done; thus it is not deception at all. "Perhaps in the past," one ethics committee member stated, "secret recordings were considered monovalent because extraordinary steps and elaborate devices were required. . . . Today, recording a telephone conversation may be accomplished by the touch of a button, and we do not believe that such as act, in and of itself, is unethical."[43]

Such recordings are an increasing part of the daily life of telephone operators, the "customer assistant" representatives of financial organizations, and the "sales associates" of catalog merchandisers. Many such organizations have decided that their employees—despite their "team spirit" and job titles that proclaim "we're a big happy family"—can't be trusted to conduct business properly and need to have their calls monitored. "This call is being monitored," announces the recording, "to ensure your prompt and courteous service." Since both sides of the conversation are recorded, it would seem that these businesses have little confidence in their customers' integrity either. With recordings, if a "dispute" or a complaint arises—from a customer or an employee—managers have the "truth" in hand.

Indeed, inexpensive computer technology is making recording a telephone conversation quite simple. With the ever-expanding use of voice mail systems, our conversations and messages are being constantly recorded and possibly stored. Many of the current generation of home computer systems have built-in voice mail–answering machine devices that can record all incoming calls (whether answered or not) and have built-in CallerID functions and other kinds of "security tools." Since these devices, like many voice mail systems, store the recorded data in digital form, a record of conversations can easily be built, passed on to others, and even edited and changed. In the cultural context of messy divorces, child custody disputes, and sexual harassment suits, the notion of "watching what you say" is taking on a whole new meaning. The same thing, of course, goes for electronic mail that many people mistakenly treat as private. This kind of correspondence is openly available to "network administrators" and others along the line, while so-called "deleted" mail is often stored on system backup tapes for quite sometime. In a recent case in New Jersey, for example, a man sued for divorce based on evidence that his wife was having a "virtual affair" with a man she had met on America Online. Evidence presented included dozens of email messages the husband obtained from the couple's own computer, which had stored the copies.[44]

HOME SWEET HOME

Increasingly, U.S. households are awash with intruder alarms and devices, video cameras, private police forces, and fenced perimeters. Taking these "security" techniques to the next level, the fastest-growing residential communities in the nation are private, usually gated, fiefdoms where, at some, visitors are videotaped as they arrive. About 28 million Americans live in an area governed by a private community association. Here the enforcement of "normalcy" is taken to new heights. These communities have a plethora of rules and regulations that govern everything from the color you can paint your house to the type of toys that can be left in your driveway. Developers and the residents appear obsessed with creating a perfect world, where all things are controlled and predicable. Here is how one journalist describes the latest model, a private suburban development near Seattle:

> There are no pesky doorbellers, be they politicians, or girl scouts, allowed inside this community. . . . A random encounter is the last thing people here want. There is a new park, every blade of grass in shape—but for members only. Four private guards man the entrance gates 24 hours a day, keeping the nearly 500 residents of Bear Creek in a nearly crime free bubble. And should a dog try to stray outside its yard, the pet would be instantly zapped by an electronic monitor.[45]

It seems no coincidence then that the Walt Disney Company, the purveyors of fantasy theme parks, is getting into the private residential development business. Its first complete city is named Celebration and is located south of Orlando.

Yet while these "serene fortresses" keep out the less desirable, some of the watching that goes on in U.S. homes is directed more at family members and others on the inside rather than at strangers lurking about outside. With the increased need for child care in the home, for example, parents often rely on near strangers to look after their children. With a string of "baby-sitter from hell" movies in the cinema and on television, paranoia runs deep in the middle-class, U.S. household. "We give peace of mind," claims the president of In-Home Nanny Surveillance, Inc., a New York City company that rents video equipment to people who want to monitor baby-sitters. He had the idea for the company when he and his working partner faced hiring a child care provider and realized that "at the end of the day, a simple referral was not enough." In business for a little over a year, he has installed dozens of cameras, but rarely has a customer discovered serious problems. "Most parents find things that are correctable. Like a nanny who smokes in the kitchen." Other companies offer several models of video cameras that are disguised as smoke detectors, boom-box stereos, and (the best-selling item, at three or four a week at the Counter Spy Shop) a teddy bear with a camera eye that feeds a videocassette recorder. Another target for the monitoring cameras, the store owners contend, are spouses who are convinced that their partners are "up to no good."[46]

Children and adolescents are particularly vulnerable to all kinds of surveillance ceremonies and techniques. It would seem that we are either frightened of other people's "dangerous" teenagers or scared of what might become of our own. For some parents, technology provides peace of mind. In addition to the cameras just mentioned, some parents turn to drug testing as a way of checking up on their adolescents (see Chapter 4). Then there is a fascinating little device called the "Drive Right" responsible-driving monitor from Davis Instruments of California. The company's print advertisement shows a contented-looking white man sitting in a chair reading. The caption states: "His teen has the car. So how come he's not worried? Drive Right uses advanced computer technology to track speed and acceleration to provide you with detailed accounts of recent driving activity." The device is capable of calculating "maximum speed and time it is reached, the # of times acceleration/ deceleration exceeded, first and last time the vehicle was moved, and the total time the vehicle was in motion." It also has a "tamper indicator and password protected settings," while "optional software connects Drive Right to your computer to create an ongoing database for each driver." In order to monitor other "deviant" activities your child may be up to, you can always listen in on their conversations. Among the hottest-selling items in electronics stores these days are telephone taping devices typically purchased by parents to monitor their kids' phone calls.

But if teenagers try to step outside the trusting confines of home, they are likely to encounter other forms of social control. More than one hundred and fifty U.S. cities now have curfews in place to restrict the movement of teenagers at night. Typically, they ban anyone under 17 from being on the streets between the hours of 11 P.M. and or midnight and 6 A.M. While instituting a curfew in Washington D.C. recently, a law enforcement official stated: "Our interest is not to go out, pick up and harass children. What we want to do is take these children out of harm's way." But curfew violators are subjected to an "automatic disciplinary process in which a violator is taken to a Juvenile Curfew Center, where a parent or guardian is notified and the teenager is counseled." One 14-year-old youth complained: "They should catch the real criminals instead of trying to keep us in the house. I don't think it fair."[47] If these techniques can't keep kids under control or "out of harm's way," there is always the option of locking them up. For most poor children and children of color, this means a trip to the local juvenile detention center. I recently attended the opening-day ceremony of a multimillion-dollar public regional facility of this kind in my hometown. Here, the emphasis seemed to be on impressing visitors that taxpayers had gotten their money's worth. We were treated to a tour that focused on high-tech gadgets like the automatic door-locking system, surveillance cameras, and the listening devices installed in the inmates' rooms. Little attention was paid to kids or their problems, however. Indeed, a representative of the

Chamber of Commerce, which hosted the event, praised local politicians for bringing much-needed dollars and jobs to the city.

Of course, if you are a white, middle-class teenager, you may find yourself shipped off to a psychiatric hospital or chemical dependency unit. During the last hundred years or so, behaviors which were once seen as instances of immorality or evil—such as drunkenness, drug use, sexual promiscuity, delinquency, and the like—have come to be reinterpreted as symptoms of sickness or disease.[48] Furthermore, increasing numbers and types of deviant behaviors are being treated in those institutions designed for the ill—hospitals and clinics—and with the sorts of psychological therapies deemed suitable to those who are seen as *in* trouble, rather than as *causing* trouble.

Running away, incorrigibility, minor stealing, and other forms of teenage "acting out" are increasingly classified through psychiatric diagnoses such as "personality disorders" and "adjustment reaction to adolescence." As I like to say, I don't know anyone who *didn't* have an adjustment reaction to adolescence! In some of my previous research, I found that there was a dramatic increase in the 1980s in the use of private psychiatric facilities to control misbehaving youth. Most of us have seen the commercials for these hospitals on TV. In most cases, they are likely profit-making operations owned by a large medical corporation and provide care and control of misbehaving or disturbed adolescents (and sometimes children) in return for third-party insurance money. Typically, kids are committed to these facilities as "voluntary" patients—after being checked in by their parents—and have no legal rights whatsoever. And, equally common, they are declared "cured" and released as soon as their parent's insurance coverage expires.

SCHOOL DAZE, SCHOOL GAZE

If kids can't be trusted to act responsibly at home, they get even less the benefit of a doubt at school. In urban and rural schools alike, the country's educational institutions are quickly becoming security fortresses where increasing numbers of children are subjected to daily surveillance rituals. In 1993, the federal government got involved, passing the Safe Schools Act, which allocates $175 million for metal detectors, security guards, and violence prevention programs. At the local level, some changes have been dramatic. For instance, after one incident with a gun at a rural West Virginia high school that left one student wounded, outraged parents demanded the resignation of the principal and forced the school to institute new security measures. Within weeks, video cameras were installed to watch kids on their buses, follow them through the hallways, and monitor their classroom behavior. They are shuttled through metal detectors and X-ray scanners operated by security guards while drug-sniffing dogs search their lockers and cars. As one journalist observed the scene, "At a guard shack outside Mount View High School, three teenagers who had been unruly on a school bus stopped for inspection recently. The guard wrote down their names and ran a hand-held metal detector over each. The youths turned on command and raised their hands over their heads." One young woman at the school, a 15-year-old, stated: "It feels like a prison in here. The older kids don't care because they've gotten use to it. But the younger ones like me are coming from schools where you're still playing with blocks."[49]

Like this young woman, my 9-year-old son echoed a similar sentiment when he came home from school one day to tell me that they had issued all the kids ID cards with bar codes on them. These devices are used in the cafeteria to tally up their biweekly bill and in the library to keep track of books and materials a child has checked out. I dropped by my son's school one day only to find him and his classmates in a silent, orderly line waiting to eat lunch, their bar-code "badges" dangling from their shirt pockets. It gave me a shudder. At the end of the cafeteria line, personnel stand with a portable computer scanning the cards and then the items that the children have selected. One staff member excitedly described the wonderful advantages of the cards: "This way we know, and can tell you *exactly* what items your child had for lunch, at *exactly* what time, on *exactly* what day!" "Gee," I said. "I guess my son will think twice about trying to sneak a chocolate milk past me again."

I have no doubt that some enterprising school administrator will get the idea to have bar-code scanners mounted at the entrances to the school to automatically take attendance and monitor the children's whereabouts. In fact, such a system may not be far off in one school district. "Just as they need a PIN number to withdraw money from an automatic teller machine," claims one journalist, "some Florida parents must now use secret passwords when picking their children up from school. No password. No kid." Officials claim the system was initiated in response to a case in which a woman lied to the school staff and fled with her niece, whom she had lost custody of. One Boca Raton elementary school principal stated that, "Everyone is so paranoid when someone comes to the office to pick up a child." Many schools in the area maintain what are apparently called "hot files"—thick dossiers on students who have been involved in custody battles or who are under state care because of abuse or neglect.[50]

As I mentioned in Chapter 1, my hometown school district was one of hundreds across the country to rotate a set of videocams throughout the district's fleet of buses. One school bus driver claims that the cameras

produced a "noticeable change" in helping her control behavior such as
the dreaded "occasional slapping match." "They'd say, 'You didn't see me.'
'Yes, I did, and the camera taped it. Do we need to play the tape?' That
was the end of it. I didn't have any more problems for the rest of the
year." The director of the district's buses says, " I think it's just the idea
that you're being watched that helps control the behavior a little bit."[51]
The children then are, like the inmates under the gaze of Bentham's
Panopticon, "awed to silence by an invisible eye."

Nationally, this trend has "just gone wild," states John Fox, a former
auto mechanic whose Texas-based company sells the camcorders and
manufactures the boxes designed to hold them. "Every school in the
United States has this problem, and it's a lack of discipline," according to
the less-than-disinterested and questionably authoritative Mr. Fox. "We
give the driver a set of eyes and the kids are dumbfounded." Interestingly,
Fox, who used to work on school buses for the Texas town, got the idea
for the cameras when he was pulled over by a state trooper who videotaped him driving erratically. Fox was not charged with any wrongdoing
but was so enamored with the technology that he thought, "Why can't we
do that with our buses?" Meanwhile a Greenville, South Carolina, school
transportation supervisor is sold on the system. "It has made a real big
difference in behavior. We had one bus where people were fighting all the
time. I couldn't keep drivers on that route. I put in our first camera there,
and it was immediate relief, like the next day."[52]

If one reads the headlines, watches the television news, or listens to
some politicians, one would conclude that our schools are decidedly
dangerous places to be. In Lawrence, Kansas, for example, a school board
member called for the formation of a districtwide "safety committee,"
claiming that we needed to be "proactive" when it came to school security. (This was the same board member who, during her election campaign, circulated an advertisement claiming that the top ten problems
reported in schools in the 1940s were things like chewing gum in class
and smoking, while in the 1990s the main problems were assault, robbery, and rape. This widely cited "study" was subsequently shown to be
apocryphal, according to the *New York Times*.) But like desperately ill
people seeking a "miracle cure," this level of "proactive" fear and suspicion can leave officials vulnerable to purveyors of "snake oil." In one
extraordinary instance, police and school authorities across the country
were recently duped by a South Carolina company selling the $995
"Quadro Tracker." This small handheld device was alleged to contain an
"indictor, conductor, and oscillator" in order to detect "molecules, static
electricity, and magnetic fields." It could, purportedly, "detect drugs hidden in air tight containers, a bomb inside a building from the outside, or
a criminal suspect from 15 miles away." Touting it like some kind of car-

toon "decoder ring," the company claimed that you simply insert "detector" cards into the machine for whatever substance one is trying to uncover. When officials at several national laboratories finally got around to testing the device, they found inside "some plastic and a sheet of paper." The FBI has declared the device a fraud and is investigating the company. One school official from a Kansas City suburb who had been convinced by a demonstration by the company to purchase the product said, "We went after this in good faith . . . with a genuine interest in trying to keep our campuses safe. And with the state of today's technology, even things that seem hard to believe, we think they can actually do these things. I'm really disappointed."[53]

But whatever the state of technology, is all this "security " and surveillance of our children really called for? In one of the final reports issued by the U.S. Office of Technology Assessment (it was shut down by a budget-cutting Congress in November of 1995), the agency concluded that children were in far greater danger off school grounds than in schools and on buses. The study's findings contradict the impression of schoolyard "war zones" that many seem to have. The director of the report stated: "We're convinced that a lot of national policy was driven not by actual data, but by fears. Any child getting shot at school is a terrible thing, and we don't want to imply that it's not. But we feel that children are in a safer environment than they would be out of school." "Schools Are Relatively Safe, U.S. Study Says," reads the less-than-sensational story as it was reported in the *New York Times*—on the bottom of page 20, next to the international weather report.[54]

NO. 2 PENCILS

But beyond the meticulous rituals children are subjected to as they move to and about school, we can't forget the classroom itself. For Foucault, the modern school represented a system of uninterrupted examination. While the stated purpose of the institution is to disseminate knowledge *to* the students, it has long been involved in ritualized knowledge gathering *about* them. Case files are built out of a series of "hierarchical observations" (surveillance, information collection, and analysis) as well as "normalizing judgments" (assessment of an individual's activity set against some standard or ideal). With increased measuring and testing, we make finer and finer gradients that distinguish one student from another. While the testers claim that they are simply better able to measure a child's innate abilities, one can argue that the tests themselves "create" the very thing they purport to measure. For example, before there were IQ tests, one wonders whether there was anything like what we consider today to be the idea of "intelligence." Before the tests, we looked at two people and said that both seemed "kinda smart" or maybe that one was "not so bright." Once they take an IQ test, however, we can claim that one is 9, 12, or 25 points "more intelligent" than the other.

From the earliest grades, the process of sorting kids into categories begins, and their educational "careers" and identities begin to take hold. The smallest details of their performance, from penmanship to their ability to sit still, are measured and evaluated. After a battery of standardized tests little Peter or Annie becomes the "slow learner," or it is decided that she has a "learning disability" or that he is "gifted" or maybe "just average." In one account by a family friend, the single mother was told that her daughter was "having problems" in the second grade. This prompted a meeting with the school's "intervention team"—a group of very well-meaning and well-intentioned professionals including the child's teacher, the principal, the school counselor, the district psychologist, a learning disabilities teacher, and a teacher of gifted children. The bad news was that the child's tests indicated that she had a "learning disability." The good news, however, was that she was also "gifted" (something that they would not have "discovered" if she had not been tested). This meant that the child was assigned an "IEP," or individual education plan, which is an even more detailed set of criteria and goals that are monitored and measured throughout the year.

An amazing example of this mentality and the whole system of "the examination"—with its case files, hierarchical observation, and normalizing judgments—is being used by a teacher at one school in our district. She is using bar-code scanning to "revolutionize tracking a student's progress." The system, called "Learner Profile," is used to build a database about an individual's academic and behavioral performance. Each category, from the smallest detail such as capitalization skills or listening skills, can be assigned bar codes with a scale of performance for each classification (e.g., "no understanding," "basic knowledge," or "mastery"). "Following the capitalization example," a journalist writes covering the story, "a teacher reads a student paper, scans the student's bar code, . . . Beep! the category, capitalization . . . Beep! . . . and say the student shows a basic understanding . . . Beep!" And, of course, "if students are interacting while she is grading, she can pause in the middle and scan in a behavior field." The teacher thinks that the information collected will be more "comprehensive" than a standard grade card that "tells us so little." She would also like to see "self-motivated students use the system, setting goals and tracking their own progress." Here, once more, those under surveillance are encouraged to use the system to monitor themselves. Asked about the distracting nature of the incessant beeping noise—but perhaps more telling about this new meticulous ritual itself—the teacher said, "I've found that they get used to it pretty quickly."[55]

Another computer software system goes even a step further, putting everyone in the classroom under the gaze. Designed by researchers at my own university, the system is intended to place a child's classroom behavior in context and "help explain why children act the way they do." The software, run on a laptop computer, is used by an "outside observer" such as a school psychologist to systematize or "impose a discipline" on observations of the classroom environment. The software "helps the psychologist silently tabulate, every 15 seconds, the teacher's behavior, the activity of the moment, the teaching materials at hand, and the configuration of the class—students working alone, one on one, in small groups." Despite the fact that one of the developers claims that, potentially, "Everything can go wrong" (such as that "people can take this, and in the worst case, use it to evaluate teachers under review"), thirteen school districts in Kansas, six in other states, and three in foreign countries are using the evaluation system.[56]

"ORDER AND CONTROL ARE EVERYTHING IN THIS BUSINESS"

"This is a controlled environment," states Ron Edens, owner of Electronic Banking System, Inc. His company processes paperwork and donations for companies and charities that choose to "outsource" their clerical tasks. Following is how one journalist described a visit to Edens's facility, an operation that may be the most extraordinary application of Jeremy Bentham's "Inspection-House" I have ever come across.

> Inside, long lines of women sit at spartan desks, slitting envelopes, sorting contents and filling out "control cards" that record how many letters they have opened and how long it has taken them. Workers here, in "the cage," must process three envelopes a minute. Nearby, other women tap keyboards, keeping pace with a quota that demands 8,500 strokes an hour. The room is silent. Talking is forbidden. The windows are covered. . . .
>
> In his office upstairs, Mr. Edens sits before a TV monitor that flashes images from eight cameras posted through the plant. "There's a little bit of Sneaky Pete to it," he says, using a remote control to zoom in on a document atop a worker's desk. "I can basically read that and figure out how someone's day is going." "We main-

tain a lot of control," he says. "Order and control are
everything in this business. . . .

But tight observation also helps EBS monitor productivity and weed out workers who don't keep up.
"There's multiple uses," Mr. Edens says of surveillance.
His desk is covered with computer printouts recording
the precise toll of keystrokes tapped by each data-entry
worker. He also keeps a day-to-day tally of errors. . . .

The work floor itself resembles an enormous classroom in the throes of exam period. Desks point toward
the front, where a manager keeps watch from a raised
platform that workers call..."the birdhouse." Other
supervisors are positioned toward the back of the room.
"If you want to watch someone," Mr. Edens explains,
"it's easier from behind because they don't know you're
watching." There also is a black globe hanging from the
ceiling, in which cameras are positioned. His labor
strategy is simple: "We don't ask these people to think—
the machines think for them," Mr. Edens says. "They
don't have to make any decisions."[57]

Extreme example? Or a sign of the times? Interestingly, Mr. Edens's
company is located in an old New England garment factory where gen-
erations of young women toiled over weaving machines and were paid
according to how many pieces they could produce in an hour. Today, the
great-granddaughters of those women struggle to make a living in what
is now an "electronic sweatshop" of the twentieth century "service economy," processing the financial paper of a consumer society and being
remotely watched and monitored by the all-seeing, all-knowing foreman,
Mr. Edens.

Now, surveillance and control have been central features of the
world of work ever since people were hired to labor for someone else. As
Karl Marx pointed out, nineteenth-century capitalism gave birth to the
central problem of modern management: how to get workers to convert
their potential labor power to labor done. In the two-hundred-fifty-odd
years since then, we have seen countless "solutions" to this dilemma,
from starvation and outright coercion, to company unions and Ford's
"five-dollars a day," to work teams and the latest prescription from this
week's bestselling management guru.

Yet, machines and technology have, in the last hundred years or so,
played an important role is keeping industrial workers "on task," controlled, and docile, thus reducing the need for supervision. This strategy
was epitomized by the emergence and evolution of the assembly line,

which brought both the production process and the workers together in a centralized system. But with the "deindustrialization" of the nation, the rise of the service industry and the "information age," the "downsizing and decentralizing of corporations, and the move toward more "flexible" use of labor, a new class of white-collar and service workers presented a fresh challenge for management. The result has been dramatic changes in the quality and quantity of watching and monitoring in the workplace and of those workers not tied to offices and desks. Workers who are increasingly using computers and other data-processing and communication technologies find that these devices become the very tools that management uses to monitor and control their movements, behavior, and productivity.

For example, at first, the "personal" computer offered us an advanced, individualized tool for doing creative work. It spawned a whole generation of "hackers" and others who celebrated such machines and their liberating potential. But corporate America was, ultimately, not interested in workers' autonomy and liberation. It wanted the productivity gains the machines offered over a typewriter, calculator, or big mainframe computer, but it also wanted to eliminate the need for constant supervision of the typing pool, of the high-priced skill of engineers, and the like. In today's workplace, the "personal" computer is no longer personal; it has been transformed into a "workstation" connected to a LAN, or local area network. Those spending their days at one of these terminals are increasingly vulnerable to managers who can use the network's operating software, according to one specialist, "to turn any employee workstation into a covert surveillance post . . . to peek at an employee's screen in real time, scan data files and e-mail at will, tabulate keystroke speed and accuracy, overwrite passwords, and even seize control of a remote workstation." In a study done by the computer magazine *MacWorld,* 22 percent of business executives surveyed said that they had riffled through employees' electronic and voice mail and files. Based on this and other findings, the magazine estimates that as many as 20 million Americans may be subject to electronic monitoring through their computers on the job.

If you enjoy cruising the World Wide Web at work, school or wherever, you may soon have someone monitoring what you are accessing. WebTrack, a new software product, is designed to "monitor and filter" Web access. You may find your favorite sites blocked; or, worse, your access may be tracked administratively. According to Stephen Dempsey, vice-president of sales and marketing at Webster Network Strategies, in Naples, Florida: "We monitor every employee's Internet activity. We log every site they have visited and how long they have spent at each site. It's a hypertext log, so the network administrator can visit that site, too. It also logs sites that were denied." Sex is only one of sixteen categories that WebTrack blocks via a proxy server that filters requests for URLs (uniform resource locators). The company has compiled a list of some 24,000 sites (updated weekly) that meet the criteria. Web administrators have complete control over which categories they care to enforce.[58]

For years, so-called futurists have been predicting that the "information age" and its associated technologies will free us from the drudgery of long commutes and the confines of the office. Today, the ideas of "telecommuting" and the "virtual office" are heralded as the means whereby we will find a new generation of happy, productive workers, who labor when and where they want. But this rosy picture has some thorns in it. While the scenario may be true for elite managers and some independent professionals, does anyone seriously think that this kind of flexibility and unsupervised work will be offered to the average worker? While the "virtual office" may not have walls—much like the "virtual prison" of house arrest has no bars—for many of the 30 million traveling businesspeople, the so-called road warriors, new telecommunications devices are becoming "electronic leashes" that keep them "wired" in and monitored. Corporate "downsizing" (i.e., massive layoffs) and decentralization, emerging global markets that demand instant availability, and a drive to boost productivity have created both demand for the more flexible use of labor and rampant uneasiness and insecurity on the part of workers. The results are that people have an anxious preoccupation with work, that they are working more hours, and that the lines between home and work life are blurring as corporations and businesses use the emerging technologies to harness workers' anxiety and enhance productivity levels.

Take the case of American Express travel agent Kathy Jones, who works out of her home in Vineland, New Jersey, more than an hour's drive from the central office in Trenton. Customers' calls are routed directly to the computer in the corner of her dining room. "It's skilled work," her supervisor told one journalist. "It can take years to do it well." But just to make sure that the "skilled" worker *is* doing it well, Jones's boss can, with a touch of a key on her own computer, look at what her agents are typing on their computers. By hitting a button on her telephone, she can listen in on any of those agents' conversations as well. But rather than calling this technology a surveillance device, management contends that it's a "learning tool." "[I]t's not used to say, 'Hey, you know, we watch what you do.' It's basically used for training purposes to say, you know, 'Looks like you have some trouble in that area. Let me get you into a class, or get you, you know, something you need to assist you with that.'" Kathy Jones seems to agree about the productive benefits of being watched and doesn't seem to mind the monitoring: "If they see you doing something on the screen that they think you can do a quicker way, they can tell you—they can advise you of it. They can even tell you ways to talk to people, or they can tell you ways to do things quicker to end your call quicker, so it's pretty helpful."[59]

Another example of the shift in the workplace was the move by International Business Machines (IBM)—the epitome of the 1950s model U.S. corporation—to sell off its massive art collection and even its huge suburban headquarters in bucolic Armonk, New York, in the wake of declining profitability. Its new approach to business is reflected in the company's purchase of a large warehouse in northern New Jersey and dividing the huge space up into small cubicles. Here, sales staff check in periodically and are assigned an "office" where they can plug their laptop computers into a network, make some phone calls, and then go back out on the road—no pictures of the spouse and kids on the desks, no time for chatting around the watercooler. With the decline of organized labor and a political movement aimed at dismantling workers' rights and privacies, the "virtual office" may take on an entirely different connotation in the future.

But it's not just office workers who are vulnerable to such monitoring. The computer and other kinds of new telecommunication devices are transforming jobs throughout the entire occupational structure. Here are some examples:

> Fran is a meter reader in California. A few years back, I encountered her darting across my backyard. I went out to greet her, curious about the small black box she held in her hand. I began to ask her how the device worked, but she said, "Gotta keep going. You can walk along though." As we moved down the street at a clipped pace, Fran told me about the mini computer she was holding. It had recently replaced the pen and clipboard she used for more than five years to keep track of electricity consumption in the neighborhood. I asked why she was nearly running between houses, and she said, "Since this thing has a built-in clock, my supervisor can now calculate how long it takes me to do a house and how many I can do in an hour. We have an average we have to keep up, and I'm behind. See ya."

> I'm at a rest stop off I-29 somewhere in South Dakota talking with Arnie who is standing next to his eighteen-wheel rig owned by one of the nation's largest trucking firms. "Hey, I hear you got a computer in your truck." "Goddam right," he says somewhat disgusted. Arnie's

computer is part of an advanced satellite communication system that permits the corporate headquarters in
Phoenix to know exactly where his truck is, within
1,000 yards, at any moment, day or night. The computer monitors his driving performance—average speed,
idle time, fuel consumption—as well as the miles he has
covered, and it will transmit to him instructions about
where he is to pick up his next load. "I have to keep that
truck as close to 58 mph as I can," he says, "otherwise
they'll bust me." He is not worried about state troopers;
he is talking about the company.

"I get twenty beeps a weekend," complains Peter Hart, a
former equipment supervisor at an electronics plant in
Freemont, California. Hart says that his job required
him to be available to the company and other employees by pager and phone twenty-four-hours a day, seven
days a week. He decided to quit his job, he says, after
pagers, cell phones, and email took over his life.[60]

Just look around. Restaurant workers are wearing vibrating "beepers" that literally prod them through their shift. Bookstore clerks are
donning wireless headsets so they can stock shelves and answer phones
and queries at the same time. Delivery people, auto-rental checkin clerks,
parking-meter readers, and a host of others are carrying data-entry computers that not only make them work "more efficiently" but also keep
tabs on their movements and/or keep track of their productivity.
Businesses are increasingly installing "card-key" entry doors that record
the activity at that access point. Since an individual's card is unique, the
door can actually tally who went through each door at what time, giving
administrators a record of movement in the facility.
　　Interestingly, at the elite, cutting edge, high-tech research center of
the Xerox Corporation called the PARC Computer Science Lab, design-
ers have turned the tools of their trade on themselves. A local computer
engineer has invented what he calls the "Active Badge": a very small
pagerlike device that emits an infrared signal every 15 seconds. Detectors
scattered throughout the facility receive the signals and feed them to the
lab's local area network, telling the computer the whereabouts of any
staff member at any time. This information is, of course, accessible at any
workstation. Olivetti Corporation is now marketing a similar device to
"insurance companies, hospitals, and other large institutions with an
interest in the whereabouts of key personnel or patients."[61]

TESTING YOUR INTEGRITY

If overt monitoring of employees through computers, video cameras, data-entry tablets, beepers, and the like weren't enough, it is likely that your employer began building a "case file" on you before you were even offered the job. In the face of what employers claim is a rising tide of lawsuits, stringent hiring and firing regulations, drug use and alleged criminal activity in the workplace, corporations are increasingly turning to preemployment background checks to screen applicants. These investigations can include a criminal records search; access to driver's-license, credit, and workers' compensation histories; and verification of educational and professional credentials, along with personal interviews with references. Of course, these kinds of extensive background checks are becoming easy to complete as more and more computerized databases come "online" and as those who control them are in the business of selling the information. Larry Craft of Datacheck Company advises employers to compare data from each record. "If an employer finds an applicant has several convictions for possessing drug paraphernalia, the employer might look at the credit report to see if the person has trouble paying their bills."[62]

Assuming you survive this kind of scrutiny, you may find yourself confronted with a preemployment "integrity test" (a favorite substitute for the lie detector which was outlawed for most preemployment situations back in 1988. I will discuss the lie detector and the drug test in Chapter 4, which focuses on surveillance and the body). Written integrity tests are used, supposedly, to measure a person's level of "honesty or dishonesty." Typically, testers will pose a set of questions that may come right out and ask whether you have committed various offenses ("Have you ever stolen products from your place of employment?"), or see what you would do under certain circumstances ("If you saw a coworker taking money from the cash register would you report it to your supervisor?"), or more subtly assess a person's values and attitudes ("Do you agree with the idea that 'Once a thief always a thief'?"). Estimates are that nearly three million of these tests are administered each year in thousands of workplaces across the country.

OK, now let's assume that you clear the background check; "pass" the integrity test, the drug test, as well as the physical; and are offered a position. Once you are on the job, your supervisor is likely to add to your "file" through an ongoing monitoring and evaluation process made infinitely more systematic and thorough than ever before with the use of new kinds of inexpensive computer software. For example, KnowledgePoint software claims that its Performance Now! package is so "remarkable" that it "actually writes your employee reviews!"

> You rate each employee on a scale of 1–5 and
> Performance Now! generates clean natural text that rec-
> ognizes strong points and addresses areas where
> improvement is needed. But that's not all; Performance
> Now! interactive advice alerts you when your ratings
> need to be backed up by concrete examples. A built in
> Employee Log helps you track examples of day-to-day
> problems and accomplishments throughout the review
> period. Increase productivity, raise morale, and protect
> your business against expensive wrongful termination
> suits.

Other packages include Employee Appraiser, which its publisher claims
is being used in 30,000 corporations nationwide. This program consist of

> more than 600 professionally written paragraphs that
> you can use in your own review documents. In includes
> a coaching advisor that offers motivational ideas and
> solutions to everyday performance issues. The Language
> Scan feature ensures you have said the right thing in the
> right way.

And then there is the WorkWise Employee File that

> helps you document performance, attendance trends,
> and benefits more easily than ever. . . . WorkWise let's
> you audit and maintain employee records (even with
> on-screen photos!). . . . Supervisors can make notes "on
> the fly" and higher management can be assured that
> employee documentation is maintained consistently
> and reliably.

Much like the bar-code system being used to keep track of the smallest details about students' behavior, software can subject workers to
minute measurements of performance; evidence can be documented and
tabulated, and penalties can be meted out when necessary. And like the
teacher who would like to see the "self-motivated students use the system, setting goals and tracking their own progress," the makers of this
software believe that the feedback provided to workers will increase their
"productivity" and raise their "morale." Interestingly, these software programs generate a kind of simulated evaluation; only the appearance of a
"real," thorough appraisal is needed to create the necessary knowledge
base. Just plug in the numbers and the program produces the sterile,
legally safe text necessary to maintain the illusion of rigor.

Now, one could argue that if you are doing your job and "keeping
your nose clean," why should you care about what's in your file? How you

do your job, your performance, is what matters, right? But what exactly does "performance" mean? On the scale between doing the minimal amount of work required and failing to adequately do your job (grounds for firing), there is a vast gray area where you may find yourself defined as a "problem employee." In fact, your boss may have just taken an American Management Association–sponsored seminar entitled "How to Legally Fire Employees with Attitude Problems: A Step-by-Step Guide." This brochure states:

Are You Stuck with Problem Employees Like These?

—Susan seems to work in only two speeds—slow and stop. She performs the minimum amount of work required, complains weekly about her workload and rushes out of the office at five o'clock on the dot every day. She makes her deadlines but you have to push her constantly. Can you dismiss her for being a *foot-dragger?*

—Tom is sharp as a tack and performs like gangbusters. The only problem is he thinks he knows *everything.* He always insists on doing things *his* way . . . openly criticizes anyone who disagrees with him, including you . . . and locks horns with co-workers every week. You've counseled Tom about his abrasive attitude but he says that *you're* the one with a problem, not him. Can you terminate Tom for being so *cocky?*

—Lisa has been whining since the day she was transferred into your department. She moans about company policies, her paycheck, her health and everything else under the sun. And when you counsel Lisa about her negative attitude, she complains to *your* boss about you. Lisa is really driving you up the wall and her negative attitude is starting to rub off on others. Can you legally fire Lisa for being a *whiner?*

As a manager, you know only too well how these kinds of employees can kill morale, add dead weight to your department and make your job a miserable chore. But can you fire workers with bad attitudes and still legally protect yourself'? The answer is YES, you can. After you attend this one-day seminar and learn the skills and techniques you need to *turn an employee's poor attitude into a concrete reason for termination,* you'll be able to fire problem employees legally, safely, and confidently. . . .

Attend this seminar and you'll learn exactly what it takes to *build your case* against employees with attitude problems. You'll learn how to *expertly document* negative attitudes and take *disciplinary action* quickly and effectively. . . . You discover how to dismiss a worker whose personality grates on everyone's nerves . . . how to legally protect yourself when conducting a termination session . . . what to do when an employee tries to intimidate you physically . . . and more. . . . (Emphasis mine)

Take the Stress Out of Firing—If you're like most managers and supervisors, you know how to fire for theft, tardiness and absenteeism, but you're not so sure how to fire for attitude. . . . Come to this invaluable six-hour course and learn the tips, strategies and guidelines you need to terminate employees with poor attitudes confidently and painlessly.

Finally, if on-the-job monitoring and surveillance are not achieved by the computer you use, the beeper on your belt, or the periodic review of your computerized "employee file," they may just be provided by your coworker in the next cubicle. "Like a lot of people who transfer to new jobs in another state," writes Ellen Schultz of the *Wall Street Journal*, "Lewis Hubble was glad to quickly make a new friend at work." However, Schultz goes on the say:

Within weeks of his arrival at the Manteno, Ill., distribution center for giant retailer Kmart Corp., Mr. Hubble, a 29-year veteran of the company, and his new friend Al were having lunch, and the occasional beer after work. . . . What Mr. Hubble didn't know was that Al was part of a married team of investigators Kmart hired to pose as employees. Over a period of seven months, the two operatives befriended co-workers such as Mr. Hubble and wrote reports about conversations in the workplace, at employees' homes, at parties and at a Hardee's restaurant. A note about conversations at the American Legion Hall included the number of pitchers of beer ordered by each employee.[63]

When the spying was later exposed by employees, it was determined that the team had reported to management things about financial and domestic problems, drinking behavior, sexual preferences, rumors about employees' sexual affairs and interoffice romances, as well as noting that one worker had "shopped at Wal-Mart."

Ironically, as workers have brought lawsuits against employers for violating the legal notion of a "reasonable expectation of privacy," some employers have adopted the strategy of informing workers, up front, that they should not expect any privacy in the first place. Indeed, some court decisions have held that employers can be found liable for invasions of privacy only if they have given their workers an expectation of privacy. "You do not want them to have a reasonable expectation of privacy," states one attorney who represents management exclusively. Instead, he said, employees should "realize if they come to the place of work, the employer is going to be opening up anything, any time, any place."[64]

CYBERNETIC CAPITALISM

No matter what discount store we shop at, the importance of our role as consumers in late capitalism is told in the story of how much energy goes into monitoring our buying habits, "lifestyle" choices, and financial stature. As I noted earlier, new forms of watching may be secured through the very products and services we are seduced into purchasing, such as cellular phones, computers, and the like. But there is far more ritualized surveillance and monitoring taking place at the very heart of our activity as consumers and as potential customers. Today, extraordinary amounts of personal, comprehensive information are collected and stored in both private-sector and governmental databases, offering easy access to this wealth of knowledge. While this kind of "social control" is clearly on the "soft side" of our spectrum, it should not be discounted as trivial. In discussing what has been called *cybernetic capitalism,* Oscar Gandy writes that this phenomenon, "increases the ability of organized interests, whether they are selling shoes, toothpaste, or political platforms, to identify, isolate, and communicate differentially with individuals, in order to increase their influence over how consumers make selections among these options."[65] This is quite a switch from a few hundred years ago. Think about it. Before the rise of modern bureaucratic organizations and their knowledge-gathering activities, the only people "known" in society were elites—heroes, villains, royalty, heads of state, and religious leaders. Everyday folks were ignored, in their day (and later by historians) in part because there were few sources of information about them. But now it seems just the opposite. Those who have social power and wealth use money to buy as much privacy as there is left and shield themselves from scrutiny. Everyone else is simply issued an account number.

The direct marketing industry demonstrates a keen watch on the American people and their habits. Marketers can purchase more than

12,000 types of mailing lists that range from, according to one account, "born-again doctors who donate," to "*Bill Moyers' Journal* transcript buyers," to "the 750,000 people who called TV's *The Jessica Hahn Show*." The "target marketing" subsidiary of the TRW credit bureau sells data about the heads of households of 87 million Americans, including their age, weight, height, ethnicity, net worth, and financial status (some of these data are gleaned from the driver's-license records that are public information in twenty states). The Behavior Bank can offer subscribers data about more than 28 million households divided into 100 different "lifestyles" based on the types of investments they have, their hobbies, and the kinds of vacations they take. Meanwhile, the Information America database contains the phone numbers, addresses, dwelling type, estimated age, and average income for 70 million Americans. Another database, called Assets, contains the property records of nearly everyone in the country, while other sources can tell someone what high school you attended and whether you have ever filed a lawsuit, filed for bankruptcy, or had a lien on your property.

Last year, in a rare move to restrict the use of these kinds of data, Missouri state officials stopped Southwestern Bell Corporation from selling businesses detailed records about the people who call them. The service, called Caller Intelidata packages the now-common CallerID information such as the date and time of each call and the caller's name, address, and zip code; the information is compiled by Equifax, Inc., a national credit reporting and information service. These additional data would include income, "lifestyle," education, neighborhood, and other census information. Southwestern Bell is already selling the Intelidata in parts of Kansas and Texas.[66] I recently dialed a customer "care" center of a national appliance company and, in addition to being told by a recording that my call might be monitored to offer me "quality assurance," I was also informed that CallerID may also be employed to "maximize" service. Meanwhile, when the *Wall Street Journal* reported that the Blockbuster Video chain was preparing to sell mailing lists of its customers, arranged by the types of movies they had rented, customers and consumer groups made it known that they were not pleased with the idea. Several days after the story broke, the company's chairman announced that the executive who had disclosed the plan had "misspoke."[67] In another case, a large food corporation used data it collected about customers through mail-in coupons and rebate forms to create a database for marketing purposes. The magazine *Consumer Reports* covered the story with the headline "Smile—You're on Corporate Camera."[68]

The General Accounting Office estimates that there are more than nine hundred federal government data sets containing personal information that are shared with other government organizations as well as with corporations and private groups. As these kinds of data become available, politicians, policy makers, and run-of-the-mill agency managers come up with new and innovative ways of using the data (and, likely, in ways that the data were never intended to be used). For example, the federal Family Support Act of 1988 mandates that states put "on line" data about so-called deadbeat parents who do not make their child support payments. These data can then be cross-referenced with other state agencies. Once this is done, welfare workers can use information from driver's license records, or even applications for hunting licenses, to track down offending parents. Or take the issue of illegal immigration. Last year, a presidential commission, chaired by former representative Barbara Jordan, a longtime advocate of constitutional rights, concluded that the problem of immigration could be addressed with computers. Jordan's commission advocated the use of a computerized national registry based on Social Security numbers. Critics charged that such a program would amount to the equivalent of a national identification card.[69]

But access to this kind of information is not just some form of "top–down" surveillance. It is one more instance where we can all get into the act as "watchers." Take a look at this offer I found on the World Wide Web:

> How YOU Can Check Out Anybody!
> The Following Information Is Provided FREE!
> Hi, my name is _____ , and. . . . As a successful businessman I have learned to always do a thorough background search on everyone that I am thinking about doing business with before I do business with them. YOU can't afford NOT to check out the guy your daughter is dating or the businessman you are about to do business with. What if that person you are about to do business with has a criminal record or is a member of organized crime?
>
> The grim specter of AIDS today makes the sexual background of your mate a matter of life and death. It is important to know about potential partners' financial assets, criminal records and sexual liaisons with members of the same or opposite sex. You need to find out if the person you or your daughter is dating really makes that much money? Does that person really have a degree? What does his ex-wife say about him? Is he a wife beater? Trust today is just naive sentimentality.
>
> Historically we used to live in small villages with little or no traveling between towns. And we would date and marry someone from the village. In old times you

knew everything about everyone else in the village. Today we don't really know anything about someone else unless you check them out. . . . Take the first step toward enhancing your personal safety and peace of mind by checking out any new person in your personal life or business. Such a "dossier" on someone is an intelligent and useful tool for avoiding a disaster or tragedy based on a person's past actions and history.

Before agreeing to meet anyone you should get their full name, age (preferably birthday), and any other information possible, e.g., license plate number, address, etc. But most important is the correct name and age which is unusually enough to build a complete dossier.

I will tell you how to check out anybody yourself. Computerization of public records in recent years has made it easy to check out anybody through a computer search of records. In minutes you can find out almost anything from home addresses and home phone numbers, marriage records, criminal records, credit information, a person's real age, ownership of businesses, history of bankruptcies, tax liens and certain medical information. Below is a list of public sources of information that you can access yourself to get information. These are the exact same sources of information that are used by private investigators in building a complete dossier on anyone. . . .

"WILL THAT BE ON YOUR CREDIT CARD?"

While advocates of privacy and immigrants' rights decry the move toward a national identification card, it seems clear to me that the vast majority of us carry around the functional equivalent of one right now. It's called a credit card. Credit cards function as a form of identification (increasingly they have our pictures on them and, very soon, are likely to have our fingerprints embedded in them). A credit card is a certificate of financial worth and an increasingly necessary key—as well as a leash—to a vast electronic financial network. You can't rent a car without one, but the police can also check your records to trace your whereabouts. As financial institutions and corporations nudge us down the road to a "cashless" society under the spell of "fast" and "convenient" service, they are building for themselves unprecedented access to our daily habits and routines. With every electronic purchase or transaction, we leave an electronic "paper trail" of our activities that can be used to build a profile of our habits and tastes and even our movements and patterns of behavior. For example, many grocery stores, gas stations, and convenience stores are increasingly encouraging customers to use checking-account cards (ATM cards) and credit cards at "the point of purchase," as it is called. In the case of grocery stores, paying with one of these cards instantly connects you to the computerized inventory of the store, which, of course, reflects the transactions of the bar-code scanner at the checkout counter. This way, a record is created of what you bought, when you bought it, and how you paid for it. These data can then be used by the store or sold to marketing firms to build a detailed portrait of your buying habits. Marketing firms are then able to "sort" you by your perceived value in the marketplace, and can ensure precise target marketing, making you susceptible to particular campaigns. (Even shoppers who pay by check can be tracked. Put in place to thwart the passing of bad checks, computerized checkout systems currently used in many national chain stores compile data about check writers, including their spending habits). If you pay cash, the transaction cannot be linked to you personally. In 1996, a major U.S. bank offered a glimpse of the "cashless" future at the Olympic Village in Atlanta, as athletes were all issued "debit" cards and no cash was accepted in the facilities. A British bank has begun a similar experiment in a small enclave in London where local merchants and all others previously handling cash are using electronic debit or "smart cards."

The consumer culture and the cashless society are due to come online as soon as the giant cable television and media conglomerates deliver on their promise to turn the nation's TV sets into "interactive" communication devices. Once every household is "wired" into these vast networks, the television will be become our primary source for new forms of multimedia entertainment, shopping for goods and services, and financial transactions. According to its promoters, the system is all about consumer choice and convenience: We will be able through our TVs to choose the programming we want to watch, when we want to watch it; to receive information about and see demonstrations of products, as well as order them instantly; and to pay our bills and make other financial arrangements. But by doing so, these and other corporations will have unprecedented access to our viewing habits, our buying preferences and choices, and our financial status as potential consumers. In other words, someone will be watching just about every aspect of our daily lives in postmodern America.

NOTES

1. Jean Baudrillard, *Simulations.* New York: Semiotext(e), 1983.
2. "For Some Convicts, Wires Replace Bars." *New York Times,* February 22, 1990: A1.
3. John E. Holman and James F Quinn, "Dysphoria and Electronically Monitored Home Confinement." *Deviant Behavior* 13, 1992: 21–32. Using a "psychometric instrument," Holman and Quinn assessed the extent of "dysphoria" (or "a generalized feeling of anxiety, restlessness, and depression") among seventy-seven clients in EMHC programs in two states. They report no significant difference between this and a comparison group of forty-nine offenders under "traditional forms of community supervision." Both groups posttested at the "high end of the normal range" (1992: 29). A student of mine told me that even being around someone under house arrest was nerve-racking. "They're always jumpy," he said. "The phone rings, and they run."
4. "New Growth in a Captive Market." *New York Times,* December 31, 1989: E12; and *Arizona Republic,* May 13, 1992: B5.
5. "New Growth in a Captive Market." *New York Times,* December 31, 1989: E12.
6. *University Daily Kansan,* University of Kansas, Lawrence, September 18, 1990: 1.
7. "For Some Convicts, Wires Replace Bars." *New York Times,* February 22, 1990.
8. Ronald Corbett and Gary T. Marx, "Critique: No Soul in the New Machine: Technofallacies in the Electronic Monitoring Movement." *Justice Quarterly* 8, 1991.
9. Michel Foucault, *Discipline and Punish: The Birth of the Prison.* Trans. A. M. Sheridan. New York: Pantheon, 1979: 200.
10. Foucault, 1979: 206.
11. A former student, who is an ISO officer, supplied this information. I must ensure the confidentiality of this individual and of the agency.
12. See note 11.
13. V. G. Hodges and B. Blythe, "Improving Service Delivery to High-Risk Families: Home-Based Practice." *Journal of Families in Society: The Journal of Contemporary Human-Services* 73, 1992: 259–65.
14. L. J. Woods, "Home-Based Family Therapy." *Social Work* 33, 1988: 211–14.Shaun Assael, "Robocourt." *Wired,* March, 1994:106.
15. Shaun Assael, "Robocourt." *Wired,* March 1994: 106.
16. Corbett and Marx, 1991: 400.
17. "Sheriff's Video Patrol Auditioning Begins." *Lawrence Journal-World,* March 6, 1994: 3B.

18. "New Police Policy Puts a Precinct on Cable TV." *New York Times,* July 17, 1994: 13.
19. "New Police Policy Puts a Precinct on Cable TV." *New York Times,* July 17, 1994: 13.
20. "New Scanners May Redefine 'Strip Search.'" *New York Times,* May 5, 1995: A7.
21. "High-Tech Crime Fighting Making Way to Kansas." *Lawrence Journal-World,* October 20, 1993: 12.
22. "Driver's License Photos Would Be Open to Police." *Lawrence Journal-World,* February 16, 1995: 4B.
23. "Ion-Scanner." *Motor Week,* Public Broadcasting System, May 5, 1995.
24. "Pot Farmer Says Agents Intruded." *Lawrence Journal-World,* June 22, 1995: 8A.
25. "In Sarajevo, Victims of a 'Postmodern' War." *New York Times,* May 21, 1995: 1.
26. "High-Tech Devices Utilized by U.S. Military in Bosnia." National Public Radio, *All Things Considered,* March 15, 1996.
27. "Clinton Gets a Wiretap Bill Covering New Technologies." *New York Times,* October, 9, 1994: 15.
28. "Privacy Issues Collide with Law Enforcement." *New York Times,* October 15, 1995: 14.
29. "New Turnpike System Lets Drivers Glide Past Lines at Toll Booth." *Lawrence Journal-World,* October 7, 1995: 10B.
30. "The Road Watches You." *New York Times,* May 13, 1995: A15.
31. "A New Way to Sniff Out Automobiles That Pollute." *New York Times,* October 22, 1995: 33A.
32. David Lyon, "The New Surveillance: Electronic Technologies and the Maximum Security Society." *Crime, Law and Social Change* 18, 1992: 159–75.
33. Lili Berko, "Surveying the Surveilled: Video, Space, and Subjectivity." *Quarterly Review of Film and Video* 14, 1992: 61–91.
34. "A High-Tech Dragnet." *Time,* November 1, 1993: 43.
35. "Thousands of Eyes for State Police." *New York Times,* May 19, 1994: A8.
36. *Lawrence Journal-World,* June 7, 1996: 6A.
37. "The Electric Arm of the Law." *New Scientist,* May 8, 1993: 19–20.
38. "Britain's Raciest Surveillance Videos Stir Outrage." *Lawrence Journal-World,* March 18, 1996: 8D.
39. "Baltimore Plans to Install 200 Cameras in Downtown." *Kansas City Star,* January 20, 1996: A20.
40. "Baltimore Installs Cameras for Public Area Surveillance." *Lawrence Journal-World,* January 20, 1996: 5A.

41. "Big Brother Enters Debate about Traffic Cameras." *Lawrence Journal-World*, February 13, 1996: 6A.

42. "Stores' Growing Use of Audio Surveillance Raises Concerns." *Kansas City Star*, May 3, 1994: D21.

43. "At the Bar: Secret Tape-Recording." *New York Times*, September 16, 1994: D14.

44. "'Virtual Affair' Leads to Divorce." *Lawrence Journal-World*, February 2, 1996: 3A.

45. "Many Seek Security in Private Communities." *New York Times*, September 3, 1995: A1.

46. "Cloak and Dagger from the Home and Hearth." *New York Times*, July 30, 1995: F8.

47. "Teen-Agers in Washington Face New Curfew." *New York Times*, July 7, 1995 : A9; "Use of Curfews Growing against Youth at Night." *New York Times*, November 8, 1993: A13; and "Philadelphia Adopts Tough New Truant Policy, with Handcuffs, Too." *New York Times*, February 9, 1994: A12.

48. Peter Conrad and Joseph Schneider, *Deviance and Medicalization: From Badness to Sickness*. St. Louis: Mosby, 1980; and Malcolm Spector, "Beyond Crime: Seven Methods to Control Troublesome Rascals." H. L. Ross, ed., *Law and Deviance*. Beverly Hills: Sage, 1981: 127–58.

49. "Even Small Schools Adding Security." *Lawrence Journal-World*, January 25, 1994: 8B.

50. "Schools Requiring ID Code to Pick Up Children." *Lawrence Journal-World*, October 30, 1995: 8A.

51. "Buses Host 'Candid Camera.'" *Lawrence Journal-World*, June 14, 1994: B2.

52. "Videocams on School Buses Becoming More Widespread." *Lawrence Journal-World*, September 11, 1993: 11A. I read a while back that in St. Louis, school authorities took another tack: They put video *monitors* on the buses, rather than cameras, and played tapes that kept the children's attention. The accompanying photo showed a row of docile students staring blankly at the screens.

53. "Drug/Weapon Finder Is a Fraud, FBI says." *Kansas City Star*, January 19, 1996: A1.

54. "Schools Are Relatively Safe, U.S. Study Says." *New York Times*, November 19, 1995: A20.

55. "Grades Go High-Tech in Cordley Class." *Lawrence Journal-World*, October 23, 1994: B1.

56. Of course, there is never any question about this being "progress." The headline reads, "KU-Developed Software Beneficial to Schools: Computer Helps in Classroom" *Lawrence Journal-World*, November 26, 1995: 8B.

57. "Mr. Edens Profits from Watching His Workers' Every Move." *Wall Street Journal*, December 1, 1994: A9.
58. "Big Brother, Web Style." *PC Week*, April 9, 1996.
59. "High-Tech Spy Equipment in the Workplace." National Public Radio, *All Things Considered*, April 1, 1996.
60. "Modern Business Technology Becoming Electronic Leash." *Lawrence Journal-World*, November 5, 1995: 6E.
61. "You're Not Paranoid: They Really Are Watching You: Surveillance in the Workplace Is Getting Digitized—and Getting Worse." *Wired*, March 1995: 85.
62. "How Deep Should Employers Dig?" *Grand Forks Herald*, February 11, 1995: 7D.
63. "Employee Beware: The Boss May Be Listening." *Wall Street Journal*, July 29, 1994: C1.
64. "Firms Walk Tightrope on Privacy Issues." *Los Angeles Times*, December 20, 1987: P4-1.
65. Oscar Gandy, Jr., *The Panoptic Sort: A Political Economy of Personal Information*. Boulder: Westview, 1993: 2.
66. "Missouri Officials Put Bell Plan—Selling Data—on Hold." *Lawrence Journal-World*, October 6, 1995: 5D.
67. H. Jeff Smith, *Managing Privacy: Information, Technology, and Corporate America*. Chapel Hill: University of North Carolina Press, 1994: 2.
68. Ibid., 3.
69. "Jordan: Use Computers to Track Immigrants." *Lawrence Journal-World*, August 4, 1994: 12.

4

Bodily Intrusions

*I'm out on patrol with a community corrections "surveillance" officer.
At 10:45 P.M. we pull into the driveway of a modest suburban house. "Pete"
walks up, rings the doorbell, and, a minute or so later, a sleepy 28-year-old
male answers in his nightclothes. Pete slips an alcohol scanner pipette to his
face, the client breathes into the tube, Pete takes his reading, says "good
night," and walks back to the car to record his findings.*
—Field notes, Staples, April 19, 1995

*Tests of eyesight, skill and intelligence hardly prepares [a citizen]
for Government demands to submit to the extraction of blood, to
excrete under supervision, or to have these bodily fluids tested for the
physiological and psychological secrets they may contain.*
—Supreme Court Justices Marshall and Blackmun
on drug testing and individual Fourth Amendment rights

I n *Discipline and Punish,* Foucault begins his history of Western social
control by recounting, in gruesome detail, the torture and execution of
a man on the scaffold in Paris in 1757 who has been accused of
trying to assassinate the king. Foucault argues that this "carnival of atrocity," this public theater, was a political ritual; a symbol of the excessive
power of the sovereign invoked against anyone who challenged his
authority. As the prisoner was tortured, he was forced to confess and
thereby set the seal of "truth" on the already-established, secret proceedings of the magistrates. The confession was an act of the criminal,
playing the role of responsible, speaking subject. The disciplinary technique of public torture, then, was an elaborate display of power and
knowledge, inscribed on the body.

But as I have argued, coinciding with the rise of the modern nation-
state, a new form of political power took hold. With Enlightenment zeal,

late-eighteenth- and early-nineteenth-century philosophers, jurists, reformers, and state authorities asserted a new discourse on crime and punishment that placed themselves as "experts" at the center of justice practice. The body of the condemned man was now the property of society rather than that of the king. Here we see the gradual disappearance of public torture and the rise of rationally organized, reformatory institutions. Within this new political regime, punishment was no longer aimed at destroying the body, but rather was intended to discipline it, to "rehabilitate" it, through meticulous rituals of power. As I have shown, this disciplinary power is advanced through the use of procedures such as the "gaze," "the examination," "hierarchical observation," and "normalizing judgments." With this modernist agenda of "rehabilitation," criminals would be understood and known in their individuality—through biography, observation, behavioral analysis—with the ultimate aim being the transformation of their "soul." Punishment would no longer breed terror and exact a public confession, it would produce deterrence and private penance.

Now, while the king could reduce an offender's body to dust or the modern asylum could watch it or train it, I want to argue that, today, there is a proliferation of postmodern disciplinary technologies that are founded on deriving knowledge *from the body*. You see, the modern regime of "rehabilitation" was premised, at least in part, on the idea of an appeal to the criminal's conscience, to what may "enlighten him from within," so that he (or she) might adhere to the social contract. Yet clearly, any behavior modification on the criminal's part was at the mercy of what we might call the individual's "privileged access" to his or her inner self. In other words, criminals had to accept their own "rehabilitation"—their new identities if you will—and change their ways accordingly. But this demanded considerable trust on the part of authorities to believe that the offender was, in fact, "a new man," and not simply on his "best behavior" while in custody.

I want to argue here that these modern ideas and practices regarding power, knowledge, and the body are changing rapidly. New developments in science, technology, and medical knowledge are making the human body infinitely more accessible to official scrutiny and assessment. The legacy of the Enlightenment continues to foster and support our almost-obsessional use of both the physical and the human/clinical sciences to treat human beings as "objects" to be analyzed rather than as speaking "subjects." Everyday we a told that researchers at universities, private foundations, and corporations have "unlocked the door" to something new about our bodies, minds, and behaviors. Yet such studies and discoveries—while they may disclose a cure for cancer or are often carried out under the guise of "intellectual curiosity" and for the "good" of human advancement—are, nonetheless, directly and indirectly, contributing to the creation and use of new disciplinary techniques for observing, manipulating, and controlling our bodies. This means that the ability of organizations to monitor, judge, or regulate our actions and behaviors *through our bodies* is being significantly enhanced. And while we see some of the most blatant examples of this phenomenon in the official justice system, we also see them at work in schools, workplaces, and other community settings.

Once put in place, these new techniques reduce the need to trust offenders to "mend their ways" or for suspects to "speak the truth" as in confessing to the use of drugs, to being at the scene of a crime, or even to having "deviant desires." Rather, it is individuals' objectified bodies that will "tell us what we need to know" and "who they *really* are" as in such categories as "known drug user," "sexual predator," or someone with a "personality disorder." In other words, it is no longer considered effective or efficient to simply gaze *at* the body—or to train it in hopes of rendering it docile—rather, we must surveil its inner evidence and secrets. I call this a "pornography of the self" because it is an obscene gaze that attempts to lay bare an individual's "true" identity. In fact, it would seem that organizations inside and outside the penal/health/welfare complex possess a raft of new devices intended to derive knowledge—or impose a form of accountability on individuals—through their bodies. And it is the social, cultural, and economic logics of late capitalism that are making this pornography of the self possible.

THE POLITICS OF "SUBSTANCE ABUSE"

This new relationship among power, knowledge, and the body is pointedly displayed in the practice of drug and alcohol testing. Meshing well with the rhetoric of the "war on drugs" that blamed the defective character of the abuser for the country's drug problem, individual testing has become the "weapon of choice" to confront the suspected drug user. Estimates are that more than 15 million Americans were tested last year—up more than 50 percent from five years ago—at a cost of $600 million. The most common location for testing appears to be the workplace, where the vast majority of the tests are used in preemployment screening rather than on current employees. However, in certain occupational categories, drug and alcohol tests can take place under conditions of "reasonable cause" (or suspicion), after an accident, before treatment, and randomly, as during preemployment. In 1994, the American Management Association reported that drug testing in the private sector has increased 305 percent since 1987, the year the association first began conducting the survey. Much of this testing was spurred on by President

Ronald Reagan's 1986 Executive Order 12564 stating that all federal employees may be tested for drugs; subsequent testing was mandated for specific occupations by the Department of Transportation and the Department of Defense. According to the latest AMA survey of major U.S. corporations, 89.8 percent of manufacturing companies tested their employees in 1993; and 30.6 percent tested periodically or at random. In the transportation sector, 87.5 percent of workers were tested for drugs, and these companies reported the highest rate of periodic or random testing, at 75 percent.[1] Today, it seems that the most common response to news reports of a plane crash, train derailment, or construction accident is: Were the individuals involved tested for drugs before or after the accident? And with the defeat of almost every civil suit brought against testing—most recently the court decision that permits the testing of public school athletes—these numbers are expected to grow.

Currently, the most common drug testing procedure involves a two-part analysis of a body fluid (typically, urine) to determine whether traces of drugs are present. The first part, a *screening test*, involves a relatively simple and inexpensive analysis using thin-layer chromatography. Under most circumstances, if the sample tests positive for drugs, a more sophisticated and more accurate *confirmation test* employing GC/MS (gas chromatography/mass spectrometry) is performed to verify the presence of the "abused substance." In addition to urine analysis, the testing of hair samples is expanding rapidly these days. The leading tester of hair samples, Psychometrics Corporation of Cambridge, Massachusetts, claims that more than five hundred U.S. corporations have turn to this method. Advocates argue that such tests "give employers a bigger and clearer picture of drug use than urine analysis can provide." This is because, when someone ingests a drug, the drug is circulated in the bloodstream, and traces of it remain in hair follicles. Since hair grows at a rate of about 1.5 inches a month, this method provides "a 90 days profile of drug use. In contrast, drug traces in urine disappear in three or four days."[2]

The simplicity and efficiency of the screening technology make the use of drug testing programs quite compelling in the world of community corrections and substance abuse programs as well as in schools, workplaces, and even homes. The commonly used urine analysis (UA) screening device consists of little more than a small plastic testing well where the body sample and reagents are mixed and the results are indicated. One manufacturer's advertising card reads:

> The Assay designed to dramatically change your drug testing capabilities . . .
>
> *Fast* setup with results in approximately three minutes.

> *Convenient* to perform on the spot, at any location.
>
> *Simple* procedure requires virtually no technical training—anyone can perform the test in just four simple steps.
>
> *Economical* testing with no equipment—a test kit and pipette are all you need.
>
> *Clear*, objective, easy-to-read "yes" or "no" results.
>
> *Reliable*—proven in clinical studies.[3]

I see drug testing much like the electronic monitoring device, as a extraordinary example of a postmodern meticulous ritual of power. The local, capillary nature of a urine analysis is clear. UA can be administered effectively anywhere; an offender need not be institutionalized to be watched and monitored. It provides instant knowledge of an individual's behavior, and codes a complex set of activities into simple "yes" and "no" categories. The device is lightweight and efficient; there is little need to collect heavy dossiers or engage in long interrogations in search of evidence or a confession. And, again, since traces of most drugs (with the exception of marijuana) are present only for one to three days after use, random rather than scheduled testing is often justified. Random screening has the effect of making this form of surveillance operate "panoptically," since individuals never know when they may be tested. In the community corrections program I observed, drug testing was done fairly routinely in the office. A screening was also conducted in the home, on a surveillance tour, when it was requested by an individual's probation officer or when Pete the surveillance officer decided to "pop them any time things don't look right." This was frequently the case with "John," a 17-year-old "heavy marijuana" user who had been caught "peeing dirty" quite often. "We can't seem to get it through his head to stay clean while he's on the program," Pete explained to me.

The drug test constitutes what Steven Nock calls an "ordeal" or a form of surveillance intended to divulge the "truth" and thereby establish or maintain a reputation.[4] But it is also a ceremony of bodily objectification, an examination, in Foucault's terms, and a disciplinary drill. Nock describes the ideal conditions under which the ritual should be performed. It is worth quoting at length, since it offers us a glimpse of the ceremonial quality of the test:

> The actual administration of the drug test is done in a controlled situation where the applicant or employee can be watched or listened to while urinating. A photo identification must be presented to verify that the individual taking the test is who she or he claims to be. To

guard against possible adulteration of the urine (many methods exist to confound urine tests), they must be conducted in such a way to eliminate the possibility of adding something to the sample, substituting another person's urine, or substituting a sample obtained during a drug-free period. Elaborate preparations and precautions are required. To prevent the applicant from concealing test-confounding substances under the fingernails, for example, the administrator of the test must witness the applicant thoroughly wash the hands. "Unnecessary" garments that might conceal things must be removed. A number of forms must be filled out to verify the chain of custody of the urine sample as it finds its way through the testing process. Both the subject of the test and the person monitoring it must fill out forms indicating that the test was I in fact, done at that time and place. The urine sample, itself, must be measured for temperature at the time of collection (to prevent the substitution of another person's urine). The sample is inspected also for color (to prevent the use of water). The urine must be kept in sight of both individuals throughout the entire process of preparing it for transmittal to the lab.[5]

During this meticulous ritual, the person being tested is forced to consent to the petty humiliation of the procedure and to the voyeuristic gaze of the tester, who must literally watch the person urinate. So while the person's "self" is embarrassed and ashamed, even, as Erving Goffman called it, "mortified," the body and its fluids, as the preceding description shows, are treated with extraordinary care. For it is the body that holds "truth," not the self. The examination is pass/fail, employing the normalizing judgment, in local terms, of being "clean" or "dirty." Moreover, the technique evokes the legitimacy of science and technical objectivity as it disassociates the client's surveillance from any particular individual. That is, it would appear that you are not really being tested by "the boss," supervisor, or your probation officer, but rather by the scientific "magic" of the test kit and the laboratory. Power is, therefore, seemingly exercised independent of the person who administers the procedure. As the maker of the testing kit described earlier states, the procedure is "useful in case-management because both you and your client can watch as results develop." Here again, those watched become "partners" in constituting the gaze upon themselves. And finally, the screening ceremony, performed enough times, becomes a disciplinary "drill." Like other surveillance ceremonies, we are at first apprehensive, unsure, and uncomfortable. But, much like the way we march through metal detectors at the airport, the test becomes routine and repetitive. Therefore, drug screening acclimates clients to accepting their own subjugation and encourages their general docility. They may even find themselves *wanting to take the test* since this becomes the only way they can prove they are indeed "clean."

Alternatively, of course, one can try to beat the test. Given the widespread use of drug testing programs, there has been a proliferation of companies that will sell "clean" urine for purposes of substitution. Hanson reports that people have attempted to alter their samples with salt, detergent, and other substances, while others have tried drinking large quantities of water or taking diuretics; in one reported case, university athletes were said to have consumed the urine of pregnant women, since they were lead to believe that this would mask the evidence of steroids.[6]

Families may be increasingly turning to drug testing to check up on their kids' activities. The Drug Alert tester, for example, marketed by SherTest Corporation, is targeted at the potential drug user in the family. You simply wipe the surface of the skin with a piece of paper and then spray the paper with the product. A representative of the company was quoted as saying that the device is intended to enhance the love and care in the home: "It's about breaking down barriers of denial between parent and child."[7] Barringer Technologies, Inc., a company that makes particle detection devices for law enforcement, created a consumer division in March of 1995 that has sold "thousands" of similar $35 testing kits to parents. The leading tester of hair samples mentioned earlier—Psychometrics Corporation—introduced a service in mid-1995 designed for parents. The $75 kit even includes instructions about how to cut the necessary sample. (The day after this product was introduced, the stock price of Psychometrics leaped from $3.00 per share to $10.50.[8]) Others products on the market claim to read a person's eye pupils and the like.

Drug testing has generated a considerable amount of litigation over the issue of privacy, but many rulings seem to follow the now-established "greater good" argument. This reasoning holds that there is a "greater good" for society established at the cost of minimal individual invasion of privacy. For example, in a case in the late 1980s the California Court of Appeals held that drug and alcohol testing of job applicants did not violate the right of privacy set forth in the California Constitution. Interestingly, the court stated:

> Common experience with the ever-increasing use of
> computers in contemporary society confirms that the
> amendment was needed and intended to safeguard
> individual privacy from intrusion by both private and

governmental action. If the right of privacy is to exist as
more than a memory or dream, the power of both public and private institutions to collect and preserve data
about individual citizens must be subject to constitutional control.

But while the court concluded that collecting and testing of urine samples in this case intruded on the applicant's reasonable expectations of
privacy, it decided that the "intrusiveness" of the drug screening was
minimal. In most cases, the court claimed, applicants are required to take
a preemployment physical exam anyway, and in this case they were
informed ahead of time that any job offer would be conditioned on consent to drug testing. Moreover, it was the judges' opinion that the collection procedures were designed to minimize the intrusion into individual
privacy (although this is not the opinion of people I talked with who
have been tested). The court concluded that the applicants have a simple
choice—either "consent to the limited invasion of their privacy resulting
from the testing" or decline the test and the job.[9]

Lately, much of the credit for a reported decline in drug use has gone
to testing programs. "Corporate programs make drug use more of a
hassle and make it seems less socially acceptable" according to one drug
program director; "There's no question they have driven down drug use."
The evidence offered for this turnaround is that the tests themselves are
uncovering less drug use. For example, in 1987, when Pfizer
Pharmaceutical, Inc., started testing job applicants, 9.9 percent turned up
positive. Last year, the company reported that the number had fallen to
3.2 percent of applicants. But, in fact, we do not know if such testing programs have anything to do with whether or not people choose to use
drugs. The lower rate may simply reflect the kinds of individuals applying
for these jobs. In arguments before the U.S. Supreme Court in the case
regarding random testing of public school athletes, it was reported to the
Court that the program in the Oregon high school named in the case
found "two or three" positive drug tests in five years it was in place. Justice
Scalia asserted that this was evidence of the program's deterrent effect,
while Justice Ginsburg claimed that one could just as easily read this as
evidence that drugs were really not a problem in the first place.[10]

CLEAN AND SOBER

As I pointed out in Chapter 3, our society has increasingly taken to
"medicalizing" behaviors that were once seen as immoral or evil. (This
phenomenon is often comically displayed on daytime TV talk shows and
"tabloid" news programs.) It would seem that in our contemporary cul-

ture, where the medical model dominates and the "sick" and "survivor" roles have become a national obsession, it is far more agreeable to be the "victim" of a disease than it is to be considered personally weak or sinful. At one time, for example, excessive drinkers were simply "drunks" who did not have the moral backbone to resist temptation. Today, these individuals are said to suffer from alcoholism, a purported medical "disease" or "addiction" that can, curiously, be "diagnosed" by family members, friends, counselors, and even judges in courts of law. Part of this transformation has been the result of medical research that suggests various underlying biological explanations for the phenomenon. But whatever physical "predisposition" there may be to abusing alcohol, drinking is primarily a behavioral activity that can be socially defined and constructed in many different ways. If we look cross-culturally and historically, we can see that what is defined as "problem" or "excessive" drinking varies widely from one setting to the next. Therefore I would suggest that much of the contemporary definition of the situation comes both from today's "victim culture" and from the people who have an interest in framing alcohol (ab)use as a problem that only they themselves as "experts" can treat. Importantly, in this context, the expert response to and the control and treatment of alcoholics has been increasingly centered on the body and on a variety of therapeutic approaches. While "excessive" drinking has been medicalized, it has also been criminalized as well. The tolerance levels for blood alcohol—the legal definition of being "under the influence"—have been lowered, while penalties for drinking and driving, for underage consumption, and for public drunkenness have increased. Between 1981 and 1985, state legislatures passed more than five hundred laws regulating drinking and driving. The result has been the emergence of new devices designed to assess the body for evidence of alcohol use and an explosion of public and private agencies geared to controlling and treating the alcoholic.

The use of alcohol is often tested by such means as the commercially available Alcoscan Saliva Test, the Final Call Breath Tester, and others. Like drug testing kits, these are quite simple portable devices that take little or no training to use. They are carried by law enforcement officials as they enable "field sobriety" checks on drivers, underage partygoers, and anyone else acting suspiciously. Another increasingly popular device is a "breathalyzer," which is installed in a convicted drunk driver's vehicle. Here the machine must be breathed into each time the person attempts to start the car. If alcohol is detected, the device will render the starter inoperable. The "ignition interlock machine" will even start beeping periodically after the car is in motion, demanding another breath test to prevent the driver from drinking after the initial test. The computerized unit records the results of each test, which are routinely passed on to probation officers and judges to assess whether the client is "backsliding" into alcohol use. Another drinking monitor has been added to the house arrest system, this one produced by Digital Products Corporation. With this device, random phone calls are breath-tested for the presence of alcohol. After calling back twice to verify a positive reading, the computer will automatically call a probation officer to the offender's home for more conventional testing.

In the community corrections program I observed, alcohol testing was used during all surveillance tours. You would hardly notice as Pete slipped the tester up to the offenders' mouths as he approached them, and they seemed quite ready for the tester to appear. Most of the clients I saw were "clean," but occasionally one would "slip up," like 17-year-old "Eric," who registered a 0.064 blood alcohol level. We drove by his house and, although Pete said he was not supposed to be home from work until 9:00 P.M., his car was in the driveway, so Pete said we would "go ahead and catch 'em anyway." "Liar, liar, pants on fire," Pete says, getting back into the car; "Claims he is taking Nyquil. Yeah, right. . . . Anyway, we tell them not to take such medication when they are on the program." Of course, all this running around the county that Pete has to do to test people for substance use is terribly inefficient and costly. He tells me that the next generation of electronic monitoring anklet devices will likely put him out of a job: they will automatically test for drugs and alcohol directly through the skin.

The enforcement of "no alcohol" under the community corrections "contract" underscores both the medicalizing and the criminalizing impact on what is, in fact, a legal substance (at least for the adults in the program). For some, it may be that program officials have decided that they are have a drinking "problem," while for others, restricting alcohol is simply part of the overall program to transform them into "productive members of society" (i.e., clean, sober, literate people who go to work and pay taxes). For those not in a community corrections program, the "road to recovery" may begin at a detoxification hospital, a rehabilitation or treatment center, a private counselor, or at the ever-present Alcoholics Anonymous (AA) meeting. While it's clear that many people have sought relief from these agencies and organizations on their own, increasingly, others may find that they have been ordered to participate in such programs under the threat of the criminal justice system. Here again, as I pointed out in Chapter 3, we see a blurring of the distinction between legal/justice and medical/therapeutic practices and discourses.

For example, for a first conviction of "driving under the influence" (DUI) in the state of Kansas, the law calls for 48 hours of mandatory imprisonment, 100 hours of community service, mandatory completion of an alcohol education program, fines of $200 to $500, plus court costs and evaluation fees, and suspension of driving privileges for 30 days and restricted privileges for another 330 days. One "community-based," for-profit treatment center is "certified by the City and District Court to provide court-ordered evaluation for DUI. . . . Following evaluation, we are certified to provide the court required ADSAP—"Alcohol and Drug Safety Action Education Treatment Program." This "evaluation" involves personal interviews with a counselor and a series of written tests designed to assess how much treatment someone requires. So it would seem that the same agency that is charged with evaluating an individual's status as a potential "problem drinker" is also in a position to benefit from the services that person is required, by law, to participate in—and the services that the agency just so happens to provide.

Another interesting example is the case of courts' ordering violators to attend AA meetings. Here we see the assumed highly effective nature of the twelve-step model as well as how a primarily therapeutic program that has existed outside the law gets colonized and linked to the system thereby enhancing disciplinary power. As most of us are aware, the AA twelve-step program has been widely emulated. It has been adapted by the spouses and children of alcoholics—the so-called "codependents" and "enablers"—as well by overeaters, the oversexed, and other assorted "excessive" personalities. But despite its popularity and significant anecdotal evidence, it has never been demonstrated, in any systematic evaluation, that AA "works." So not only are courts ordering people to participate in something they cannot say is effective, but, at a minimum, it brings into question the idea that this is anything like "self-help." In this context, the twelve-step program becomes a disciplinary technique that provides a monitoring, surveillance, and social control function for the state.

THE "TRUTH" MACHINE

The availability and proliferation of drug and alcohol testing relieves workplace supervisors, athletic-team coaches, justice officials, and others of the tedious task of interrogating suspects while ritualized, random testing may offer a significant deterrent effect. But what if we think someone has stolen money from the cash register, sold industrial secrets, or just simply isn't telling us what we want to hear? Deciding whether someone is lying has been the responsibility of another technology of bodily "truth," the polygraph. The idea behind this device dates back to Italian criminologist Cesare Lombroso (1836–1909) (who, incidentally, asserted that criminals are born with certain recognizable hereditary physical traits such as skull size). During the midnineteenth century, Lombroso began taking measurements of the blood pressure and pulse of suspects under interrogation. The technique was later "refined" in the United States; the first portable polygraph machine was developed in the 1920s and was used extensively in criminal investigation. By 1987, one government agency estimated that as many as 2 million test were being done each year in the United States. And, in a wonderful postmodern twist, the most popular television show in Spain today is called *The Truth Machine.* Styled after a failed 1980s U.S. show starring F. Lee Bailey (one of the famous lawyers who defended O. J. Simpson), this successful nine-ty-minute drama subjects politicians, businesspeople, and celebrities who have been accused of assorted infractions to the test so they can attempt to prove their innocence. One show included American John Wayne Bobbitt, who, when asked whether he had beaten his wife the night she cut off his penis, recorded "significant deception" on the test.

Like the drug test, the polygraph evokes an extraordinary ceremoni-al procedure. Most of us have watched the scene in the cinema at one time or another: A blood-pressure cuff, attached to a sphygmomanome-ter, is first wrapped around the suspect's upper arm. Then two tubes are wrapped around the person's upper and lower chest to measure any changes in respiration. Finally, two electrodes are placed on the index and second finger of one hand; these will assess any changes in the per-son's perspiration level. Data from these sensors are displayed to the examiner on a rotating paper chart, showing changes as spikes, peaks, and valleys, much like an earthquake monitor. The theory behind this is that, when a suspect is questioned about his or her activities, a "lie" will be detected by increases in blood pressure, respiration rate, and the like.

The polygraph, like the drug test, is a portable machine that can be set up anywhere. And here, once more, the remarkable power of science and objectivity is conjured up to authenticate the "true self." As Hanson claims, "Some polygraph examiners, in an effort to heighten subjects' perception of the test as a professional procedure, go so far as to wear a white coat, stetho-scope dangling from the neck, and to spray the air of the examining room with ethyl alcohol."[11] Yet the lie detector is a charlatan. Its use has never been shown to accurately discern fact from deception.[12] Indeed, polygraph evidence is rarely admissible as in a court of law. When CIA agent Aldrich Ames was asked about how he managed to pass several agency lie-detector tests during his years as a Russian mole, he replied, "Well, they don't work." Indeed, even the U.S. Congress was so convinced of the fallibility of this technology that in 1987 it passed the Polygraph Protection Act, which out-lawed the test in preemployment situations. The statue defines *lie-detector test* broadly to include polygraphs, deceptographs, voice stress analyzers, psychological stress evaluators, and similar devices.

If the polygraph is indeed so seriously flawed, despite its "scientific" underpinnings, one could ask, Why is it used at all? The lie detector functions quite nicely in most situations as a way of coercing confessions and as a general form of surveillance. It does so by creating the illusion that the truth can, in fact, be had. Yet the "truth machine" is all smoke and mirrors; it generates knowledge through the simulation of the objective power of science. Since most people are not aware of its flaws and do not know how to "trick" the machine, they are likely to be very intimidated by the process. Like the black spot of the inspector's lodge of the Panopticon, the lie detector leaves people uncertain about what it is capable of knowing. As one writer put it:

> If a subject believes that the ordeal works . . . there is strong incentive for the guilty to confess. The ritual aspect of the polygraph ordeal (the pretest interview, the connections of electrodes and straps to the body, the careful repetition of questions over and over) . . . sensitizes subjects—it frightens them. It helps convince them that there is no hope in fooling the ordeal. It makes lying seem senseless.[13]

It is said that it is often the case that individuals subjected to this ceremony are so terrified by its purported ability to reveal their inner secrets that they confess to activities having nothing to do with the present questioning or, incredibly, to crimes they are, in fact, innocent of committing. The disciplinary ritual is, therefore, capable of "creating" the very phenomena it seeks to uncover. Used judiciously, then, lie detectors may encourage self-surveillance and function as a deterrent to acting or behaving "inappropriately." In a culture where "everyone is so paranoid," disciplinary ceremonies like the polygraph remain popular devices despite the laws that prohibit their use. Last year, for example, following on the heels of the case of Susan Smith—the South Carolina woman who rolled her car into a lake, drowning her two children strapped into their car seats—the Justice Department issued a 220-page guide for law enforcement officials investigating the cases of missing children. The report, written by the National Center for Missing and Exploited Children, claims that the police should assume that any child missing is in immediate danger and that they should search the home, even if the child has been reported missing from somewhere else, and they should quickly give the parents a polygraph test.

DEVICES AND DESIRES

Recent developments suggest that even our most intimate, private thoughts may be available for official scrutiny. Based on some of the same principles as the polygraph, that is, the measurement of the flow of blood to a limb, the *plethysmograph,* or "p-graph," is a narrow metal or rubber band that is placed around the penis of a male subject. The individual is then forced to watch visual displays of naked adults and children or, sometimes, to listen to audiotapes. The band, of course, measures variation in the circumference of the penis. The accompanying computer software enables the examiner to know which stimulant produced an arousal and the relative degree of the erection. Use of the p-graph has been a favorite technique among sex therapists for more then twenty years, and it is now commercially available and aggressively marketed by several manufacturers. The president of the leading producer of the devices, Farrall Industries, Inc., contends that the device is, indeed, capable of "accurately measuring sexual desire" but that it cannot determine whether someone has committed an offense or is likely to do so in the future. The p-graph is presently being used in over four hundred sex-offender treatment centers in forty of the United States and in several countries around the world.

Yet the mechanism is, according to one article, "emerging from behind the locked doors of adult treatment centers and into the broader legal arena" and is turning up in sentencing and parole decisions, custody fights, and the like. For example, fathers are being subjected to p-graphs in child custody disputes as lawyers seek to prove that they are—or aren't—likely to abuse their children. In a case in New York, a psychologist used the p-graph on a father whose parental rights the county was trying to terminate. He concluded from the test that the father "did not become sexually aroused by either male or female children." But an expert witness for the county disputed the findings on the ground that the test could not predict any potential behavior. At a hospital in Phoenix in 1992, boys as young as 10 who were accused of abusing other children were tested with the p-graph. The law seems ill-equipped to deal with questions of privacy and rights since there are no regulations regarding the devices at this time. One therapist acknowledges that "a majority of people who undergo the assessment would prefer not to go through it. It's measuring the one thing left that is supposed to be private."

In an extraordinary case in Maine, a police officer whose name was simply raised in a local sex-abuse case was told he had to submit to a p-graph as a condition of keeping his job. In a bizarre string of accusations, Officer Harrington was one of 170 other people, including a U.S. Senator, who were accused of sexual impropriety by four siblings. While no legal evidence was ever brought against him and he was never formally charged, the district attorney said he had "doubts about the man's character" and wanted "to be sure that the officer didn't have deviant thoughts that might lead to dangerous behavior." As Foucault put it, when one wishes to create a "case" out of the "healthy, normal and law-abiding adult, it is always by asking him how much of the child he has in him, what secret madness lies within him, what fundamental crime he has dreamt of committing."[14]

Harrington was ordered to see a sex therapist, who requested that he take a sex-offender profile test as well as the p-graph. The written exam determined that Harrington's "personality profile" was supposedly similar to that of about 6 percent of sex offenders. He later refused to take the p-graph. Some in the town suggested that this was a sign of guilt, but some two thousand others began a petition drive to support him. Three years after he was accused, Officer Harrington still had not gotten his job back and was filing a federal lawsuit against the town.[15]

REGULATING SEX AND TESTING FOR AIDS

"Dangerous" sexual behavior may also be a factor when authorities confront a disease such as *acquired immune deficiency syndrome,* or *AIDS.* Currently, more than a million Americans are infected with the HIV virus that causes AIDS, and more than 200,000 died of AIDS-related illnesses last year. To date, estimates are that 1 in every 93 young men between the ages of 27 and 39 may be infected. Since AIDS first appeared in the male homosexual community in the United States (as opposed to the sexually active heterosexual population in Africa, for example), public health officials and politicians have had to involve themselves in what the *New York Times* called "The Indelicate Art of Telling Adults How to Have Sex."[16] What concerns health officials the most are public meeting places like bars, bathhouses, and swingers' clubs, where people go to have sex. While such places are legal, most fall under and are regulated by the health department. In most states, health codes prohibit a list of sexual acts from taking place in commercial facilities. Yet, medical experts argue that the crucial factor in AIDS transmission is not a matter of what kind of sex you have, but whether or not participants use a condom. So the question of just how much "regulation" is to take place pits public health protection against civil liberties and personal freedom. Advocates of protecting the public contend that "reasonable intervention" involves education and inspection of businesses to see whether violations are occurring. Civil libertarians, on the other hand, argue that the government, besides making information available, has no business, particularly at taxpayers' expense, telling adults how they should have sex.

But officials worry that the sex clubs—that have both homosexual and heterosexual patrons—are a particular danger because their customers tend to be young adults, men who have sex with men but who do not identify themselves as gay, and visitors from out of town who may not be aware of prevention practices. In most cities, club owners have the responsibility of making sure that "high-risk" sex does not occur in their clubs; some hire "monitors" who patrol the premises, while others require patrons to sign a written pledge to use condoms. In New York, in order to make sure the clubs are in compliance, a dozen health inspectors are trained to do "spot checks." They are assigned to look for monitors and to see that the business itself is watching customers. "Closed rooms and poor lighting would raise a red flag," according to one journalist.[17]

The AIDS epidemic has also brought about the thorny problem of mandatory testing for the disease and issues regarding the privacy of test results. The questions have arisen in a variety of settings. In the workplace, owners and mangers fear the spread of diseases in their organizations and the potential for lawsuits against them. On the other side, workers, particularly those in "high-risk" occupations, fear contamination by the public they serve; while others, who may be contaminated themselves, worry about possible discrimination or losing their jobs or their insurance if test results are made available. The case of four Floridians who claimed they contracted AIDS at their dentist's office brought calls for the testing of all health care workers. Later, medical, labor, and advocacy groups along with the Centers for Disease Control argued that such testing made little sense, since it is health care workers themselves who are more likely to be exposed to the disease from their patients. Olympic diver Greg Louganis spurred calls for mandatory testing of athletes when he announced that he had AIDS and that he had tested positive for the human immunodeficiency virus (HIV) before the 1988 Olympic Games. Louganis bled after cutting his head on a springboard during competition in the 1988 games. Others have called for mandatory testing of boxers as well as other athletes.

Meanwhile, some in the medical community and public health advocates called for a law to compel pregnant women to be tested for the HIV virus and then, if they test positive, to be required to undergo AZT drug therapy to help save their unborn children. Proponents argued that pregnant women must be tested for venereal diseases and that there is no reliable means of preventing the transmission of the virus to the child. During its 1994 session, the New York state legislature passed legislation mandating HIV counseling for all pregnant women but stopped short of authorizing hospitals to test infants without their mothers' consent. The state's medical community came out against mandatory testing, arguing that more children's lives would be saved through testing with the mothers' consent. When a man facing twenty-four charges in the rapes of six women went on trial in California in 1993, his alleged victims were issued notices from county health officials that they may have been exposed to the HIV virus. Health officials, however, would not reveal whether the man had tested positive or not, citing the state's confidentiality law, which protects the identity of people who test positive for HIV. In Nebraska, a U.S. Circuit Court held that a mandatory HIV testing program of a state agency serving the mentally retarded violated the employees' Fourth Amendment right against unreasonable search and seizure. This case challenged the constitutionality of the agency's chronic infectious disease policy, which required HIV and hepatitis B tests of all employees in positions involving direct contact with clients. Yet in another case, a federal district court upheld the permissibility of AIDS testing of a health care worker whose long-standing roommate was admitted to the hospital and diagnosed as having AIDS.

A disease like AIDS demonstrates how the body is becoming a contested terrain in the battle over questions of individual privacy and organizational demands, be they schools, hospitals, workplaces, or public health departments. The social control implications of the battle are clear, however. As Dorothy Nelkin and Laurence Tancredi state in their book *Dangerous Diagnostics:*

> Institutions must operate efficiently, controlling their workers, students, or patients in order to maintain economic viability. In some cases social controls are explicit, exercised through force; but more often institutions seek to control their constituents less by force than by symbolic manipulation. Sanctioned by scientific authority and implemented by medical professionals, biological tests are an effective means of such manipulation, for they imply that institutional decisions are implemented for the good of the individual. They are therefore a powerful tool in defining and shaping individual choices in ways that conform to institutional values.[18]

VIRTUAL IDENTIFICATION

Clearly, advanced capitalism is engendering rapid technological developments in the intersecting field of forensic, medical, and computer sciences that are creating new forms of body-based evidentiary and archival knowledge. For years fingerprints and dental records were used in criminal investigations and courtrooms. Yet today, not only have these sources of evidence become far more sophisticated and more proficient, but they also are creeping outside the bounds of the justice system. For example, in 1990, the FBI began converting its 40 million fingerprint cards and crime-history records into digitized files, creating a huge centralized computer database. This database includes not just the files on previously convicted criminals but also the prints of ordinary citizens who apply for federal jobs or special licenses. Law enforcement agencies in thirty-nine states, the District of Columbia, and some 350 towns are adopting optical-reader fingerprinting systems like those sold by such companies as Digital Biometrics, Inc., which will be linked to the centralized data sets. Even mobile scanners, used on the street, are not far off, according to one FBI official.[19] "We scan prints from all 10 fingers and initiate a search of the other known offenders to see if the person has been arrested before but under a different name," one police official said. "You cannot imagine the pleasure it gives you to go to that person arrested on a DWI and say, 'You want to tell us about that murder a few years ago?'"[20]

But such dramatic,"feel good" stories from the world of law enforcement conceal the more mundane encroachment of these kind of techniques and databases in the public arena. Both California and Texas are now taking a thumbprint of every person simply issued a driver's license. In fact, in Texas, if you try to cash a check at a bank where you do not have an account, you must now offer your thumbprint to a scanner and place another copy of it on the check. Los Angeles County was the first to begin taking fingerprint images of all welfare recipients; authorities expect the practice to be universal in a few years. The county's slogan for this program is "Fingerprints for better service," and it expects to save $18 million by preventing fraudulent claims over the next five years (minus the $10.8 million needed for staff and equipment). Yet a spokesperson for the U.S. Department of Health and Human Services asserts that there is no empirical evidence that fingerprinting is an effective means of preventing welfare cheating. So why invest all this money and create a new system of potential surveillance and social control? The head of New York State Social Services asserts that fingerprinting is mostly to satisfy the widespread feeling among the general public that they are "being taken" by "welfare cheats." "The public has the perception that the welfare system is rife with fraud," he said. "It is a wrong impression."[21] One has only to listen to the rhetoric of the latest political campaign or a so-called investigative news program to see how that misconception has been created.

In addition to traditional fingerprinting, biomedical information about individuals is being derived from tissue typing; hair, blood, urine, and semen analysis; voice imprints; the "reading" of eye pupils; and the like. For example, one company, Personnel Identification and Entry Access Control, has devised a new system of identification that is based on the measurement of the human hand. It has spent more than $2 million developing the machine with grants from the state of Ohio as well as from the U.S. Air Force. The president of the company, a medical physicist, said he is marketing the device to makers of automated teller machines as well as to companies and organizations that want to restrict access to high-security areas.[22]

A British firm, EDS Scicon of Surrey, has designed software for a computer-driven video system called Sentinel that can detect objects of a particular size stopping in the region on the camera (e.g., a human shape). It then automatically turns the camera on and records the movements of, say, everyone leaving a certain door of a building and indicates what direction each person is headed. A similar system being installed in the Sydney, Australia, airport will be able to recognize and identify an individual's facial characteristics and compare them with those in a database. Back in the United States, Iterated Systems of Atlanta, Georgia, uses fractal processing to break down facial images for identification and storage.

IT'S IN THE GENES

Another form of bodily identification and evidence that was made a central feature in the infamous O. J. Simpson trial is what has been commonly referred to as "genetic fingerprinting" (although courts prefer the less precise term "genetic profiling"). Here an individual's unique genetic material, DNA, which is found in all human cells, may be used as evidence of criminal involvement. The FBI has initiated the *Combined DNA Index System*, or *CODIS*, a national DNA identification system. Kansas, for example, was selected to be part of the program, and, under a law passed by the state legislature in 1991, samples of blood and saliva from several thousand individuals with criminal records have been collected to date. As many as fifteen other states have joined in and collected thousands and thousands of samples. In the state of South Dakota, simply being arrested brings about a DNA test.

With the approaching conclusion of the Human Genome Project, an international effort by scientists to "map" the entire set of genes comprised by human DNA, more will be known about the human body and how it functions than ever before. In this context, genetic material will become increasingly important, and a determining factor, in assessing an individual's predisposition to diseases and even certain personality traits and their assumed links to behavioral patterns. Organizations such as workplaces, schools, hospitals, insurance companies, health and welfare agencies, courts, and those involved in law enforcement will all have increasing incentives to store and use this kind of information.

As with many medical discoveries, knowledge, and tests, we seem ill-prepared as a society to deal with the social, legal, and ethical implications of DNA evidence. While the use of such material in the criminal justice system is taken as perfectly legitimate, its uses in other spheres of life seems questionable. For example, genetic testing in the work place can take the form of screening employees for susceptibility to disease or of monitoring employees to determine the extent of damage caused by workplace exposure to hazards. Once the data are available, individuals could be subject to genetic discrimination in employment based on test results. A worker's privacy could be undermined through the compilation, storage, and release of non-job-related, sensitive medical information. Finally, the fear of employment discrimination through employer's access to genetic records might discourage certain individuals from undergoing needed genetic testing.

To date, at least nine states have passed legislation limiting insurers' ability to genetically test applicants for insurance coverage purposes. In Minnesota last year, two legislators introduced a bill known as the Genetic Discrimination Act to try to stop insurance companies from screening out people who have not even been diagnosed with a disease. A similar bill was passed in California the previous year. The two lawmakers in Minnesota argued that some people in the state were afraid to undergo tests that could reveal whether they carry the gene for a particular disorder because if the test is positive they may be unable to get health, disability, or life insurance. "If we don't pass this legislation now, it's very possible that we'll create a genetic underclass in this country for whom insurance is impossible," a legislator argued. But the insurance industry in the state fought the bill. A representative of the industry claimed: "This is anti-consumer. It is unfair to consumers to prohibit insurance companies from underwriting policies based on the best available information."[23] A 1993 American Council of Life Insurance study revealed the degree of mistrust among the public: 56 percent of those surveyed felt that insurance companies could not be trusted to keep the results of genetic tests confidential.[24] In 1993, the federal government's Task Force on Genetic Information and Insurance concluded that the rapid expansion of predictive genetic testing would result in an explosion of information about genetic health risks and that risk underwriting should not determine access to health care.

In 1996, two marines in Hawaii filed a lawsuit that could have a profound influence on the way our society handles genetic information. The marines are refusing to provide blood samples for the Defense Department's DNA databank, a collection of DNA samples that are to be used to identify the remains of soldiers. The marines say they're concerned that genetic information about them will be used for other purposes. The use of genetic material as evidence in civil as well as criminal legal cases is expanding. For example, in California, a county judge decided to require a mentally retarded teenager to undergo genetic testing for evidence in a product liability lawsuit. The request came from a chemical supplier accused of causing the teenager's condition. DNA material is being use to circumvent a previous Supreme Court ruling that bars paternity actions against dead men. In what might be called "Who says dead men can't pay child support?" lawyers for plaintiffs argue that if the identity of an illegitimate child's father can be established, even in the absence of the father, motions against the property and the right to be supported can be claimed by the child. In 1994, a Connecticut judge ordered blood testing in a civil medical malpractice action against a psychiatrist accused of having sexual relations with a patient.

Given the powerful implications of genetic knowledge, some suggest that, within a few short years, most of us will have our DNA profile on record somewhere. As the authors of the book *Dangerous Diagnostics* put it:

> The social meaning of this information in the 1990s must be reconsidered in the context of an increasing sense of crisis—over criminal violence, the cost of heath care services, the quality of education and the general state of the economy. . . . These economic and social imperatives are enhancing the social value of predictive testing and reinforcing the power of biological information well beyond the clinical context.[25]

AUTOMATED HISTORIES

This sci-fi world of DNA databanks, will, however, be built on the vast information network that is already in place. Most of us have little idea how much personal and medical knowledge about us is floating around in computerized databases: corporate personnel files; hospital, mental health, and substance abuse agency records; and insurance company databanks join all those demographic, financial, credit, and consumer-habits data I covered in Chapter 3). Much like the case of detailed employee review and evaluation files, this systematic monitoring and knowledge-gathering activity is being advanced by the use of relatively inexpensive computer technology. For example, take the software package called *Automated Social History,* marketed by Anderson Publishing Company. An advertisement card for the product shows a series of ten identical human heads, each turning from front view to portrait, and each drawn in a kind of fractal, geometric design that evokes a scientific "gaze" on the skull. The card states that the software provides an

> efficient and professional way to produce narrative social history reports . . . encompassing the most impor-

tant areas of the subject's social and personal functioning. The program screens the subject for major forms of
social, psychological, psycho-neurological, and medical
illness. . . .

Completion of the ASH Plus questions generates
five useful reports:

> Narrative Report. *Used when a comprehensive social
> history is needed, this summary covers 13 areas of a
> person's life: religion, parents, family, education, mar-
> riage, personality traits, interests, sex, military,
> employment, crime history, alcohol/drug abuse, and
> medical history.*
>
> Self-Reported Personality Traits Report. *Provides an
> interpretation of the subject's self-description.*
>
> Items Report. *Produces a chart of the actual item
> responses to all questions administered.*
>
> Risk Analysis Report. *Produces a weighted risk
> analysis which can be used for any prediction scheme.
> . . .This report can be extremely useful in proba-
> tion/parole prediction. Can be utilized when deter-
> mining the length of stay in residential substance
> abuse programs.*
>
> Summary Report. *A clinical summary weighing
> behaviors and attitudes that may contribute to the
> subject's current problems. This report infers a quick
> review and index of the current problems.*

And, much like Bentham, who argued that the Panopticon could be
adapted to fit a variety of institutional settings, this company sees wide-
ranging uses for its product. "Who should use ASH Plus?" they ask, and
then provide the answer: "Physicians, Psychologists, Social Workers,
Hospitals, Mental Health Agencies, Substance Abuse Agencies, Probation
and Parole Agencies, Correctional Institutions, Court Systems, and
Security Departments."

With corporations "downsizing" in the context of a national health
care crisis, businesses are looking for places to cut costs while insurance
companies are seeking as much information about prospective claimants
as they can get. The result is new techniques and technologies designed
to assess a person's physical, mental, and emotional health and to collect
and store the information provided. For example, a growing number of
Fortune 500 conglomerates is turning to so-called behavioral health care
companies to oversee the mental health care and alcohol and drug treat-

ment programs of their employees. Marketers like these are selling a new system of measuring mental health care treatments and their effects. Rather than rely solely on a mental health workers' experience or training to develop a treatment plan, new clients are asked to answer a battery of questions designed to assess their symptoms, state of well-being, familial relations, and the like.

These data and the assessment of the therapist are entered into a computer software program that compares the symptoms of the new patient, say for depression, with an extensive database of hundreds of similar cases. It also compares patients with a "standard of normal behavior" based on studies of healthy people. By having detailed data on other patients—how they were treated and what the results or "outcomes" were—a therapist can then follow a similar line of treatment with the new patient. A "case reviewer" at the company sends the therapist a simple chart that shows how the patient's symptoms compare with both the previously ill and the normal range of behavior. These charts may be shared with the patients "to compare the ups and downs of . . . symptoms with the standard of normalcy" so that they might understand the extent of their problem. After the therapist arrives at a course of treatment, similar charts are produced after every sixth session, based on new questionnaire data. Research in the field of "outcomes" in mental health care have been fostered by federally funded studies and by large insurance companies, hospitals, and health maintenance organizations that are "sifting through their own enormous files, analyzing the results of their treatment." A "pioneer" in the field, Dr. G. Richard Smith, a psychiatrist at the University of Arkansas, states that now "we are able to measure many more aspects of mental health care then anybody dreamed of five years ago."[26]

HOW ARE WE FEELING TODAY?

The area of medical records seems particularly vulnerable to privacy abuses, inaccurate data, and questionable insurance practices. Data "brokers" such as the Medical Information Bureau sell medical records to businesses and insurance companies so that they may determine whether a potential employee has a "preexisting condition" that warrants special consideration. Such information may be used to screen out potential "high-risk" employees and expensive claims. According to one journalistic account, such files often contain not only information about previous medical treatments but also whether a person has sought psychiatric help, been treated for substance abuse, and even if he or she engages in "high-risk" leisure activities such as hang gliding.

With increasing importance placed on medical data, even sharing details about your personal life on the job may come back to haunt you. While it is not likely that your coworker is a company spy, he or she may still be a source of information particularly if the boss decides to challenge claims for medical or disability benefits. In one case in Oregon, a secretary who filed for compensation from repetitive motion problems was surprised to find that, at a hearing, lawyers for the insurance company claimed her problem was caused by emotional stress and hormone fluctuations resulting from an abortion. "I had no idea that things you tell your friends in the office can be used against you," she said. But this "happens all the time," according to Pam Wear, a former director of a medical records trade association; "Sharing your personal lifestyle can be dangerous to your medical coverage." Pinkerton Security and Investigation Services and Wackenhut, Corporation offer their clients—companies like Northern Telecom, Merck & Company, Boise Cascade, General Motors, and Allied Signal—toll-free phone lines, operated twenty-four hours a day, to encourage workers to "pass along accusations that their colleagues are using drugs, drinking, stealing, committing medical fraud or engaging in other illegal activity."[27]

Companies themselves are collecting vast amounts of detailed medical data on their employees. Each year American companies require employees to submit to millions of blood and urine tests, X-rays, and other medical and laboratory procedures. Not only are files built during preemployment physical and routine checkups, but some employers are using data collected in their "wellness centers" to confront employees' claims for benefits resulting from workplace injuries or stress. Workers often fail to realize that such medical records are not fully protected by doctor-patient confidentiality. For example, Adolph Coors Company in Golden, Colorado, operates a 23,000-square-foot wellness center devoted to keeping workers healthy with exercise programs, on-site medical personnel, and a counseling center. Coors estimates that by providing this "benefit" to employees the company saves $2 million a year by cutting sick leave and medical costs. But is also offers management a detailed source of medical information about their workers. Consider the example of longtime employee Richard Truman Fletcher. His case was described by *Wall Street Journal* reporter Ellen E. Schultz:

> The company knew he had the mumps at age eight, had lost his left eye in a fireworks accident at nine and had a vasectomy in 1962. It knew he smoked 30 cigarettes a day. It even had a note in its files saying he was embarrassed by smelly feet. One day in 1992, Mr. Flectcher died of a heart attack at the age of 54. His wife, Judy, filed for survivor's benefits. . . . The widow thought she had a

strong case. Her husband had died two weeks after being demoted from a desk job to manual labor. . . . But Coors argued that Mr. Fletcher died from smoking—and all it had to do was flip open his extensive medical files to make its case. Coors had no need to hire a subpoena-wielding lawyer to go on a fishing expedition in hopes of finding a doctor to testify or a written record to bolster its position. It already knew that Mr. Fletcher had smoked a pack and a half a day since age 14—enough to persuade an administrative law judge to deny the widow's benefits.[28]

But the biggest saving, Schultz goes on to point out, comes from using the data to identify costly benefits that can be reduced, or to shift costs to employees. She cites, for example, the case of Hershey Foods Corporation, where workers now pay an extra $30 a month for health insurance if they have high blood pressure, $10 for high cholesterol, $10 if they don't exercise, $50 if they use tobacco, and $30 if they are over-weight. Hershey caps the total of such extra charges at $840 a year per employee; the testing is mandatory. The data can therefore be used, according to one consultant, so that "management can now forecast where the ticking time bombs are in their employee population." Last year, a New York electronics firm began charging these so-called time-bomb workers higher premiums, instantly shifting $232,000 of health care costs to employees. The 20 percent who refused to take the wellness test were charged the highest premium. "They were either smokers or had some condition they're trying to hide," said a company representa-tive; "Now we need to evaluate the people with something to hide."[29]

NOT MY BOSS . . .

But what do workers think of all this? Despite such incidences as those cited, workers appear to think well of employers. A survey of 1,000 work-ers of private-sector companies that hire 15 or more people conducted by Louis Harris and Associates in 1993 indicated a relatively high degree of employee confidence in employers' collection and use of personal information. In this poll, 90 percent of the employees surveyed believe that their own employer had never asked for personal information that was inappropriate or not employment-related. Moreover, 61 percent of those asked said that they believed their employer respected their off-the-job privacy and had not collected inappropriate information about them. Yet, at the same time, 79 percent of the respondents were general-ly concerned about threats to their personal privacy. It would appear that, at least for these workers, such threats could not happen in *their* workplace.

Interestingly, the survey also included a comparison group of 300 corporate human resource executives. Both groups, it would seem, had similar attitudes about what types of tests were appropriate for employers to use in making hiring decisions. Among the practices both sets of respondents cited as "improper" were tests for nicotine use off the job (93 percent of employees, 95 percent of executives); genetic blood tests (88 percent of employees, 93 percent of executives); urine tests for alcohol (69 percent of employees, 66 percent of executives); and HIV-antibody tests (57 percent of employees, 73 percent of executives). Furthermore, 89 percent of the employees in companies that conducted alcohol and drug testing believed that such testing was a good idea.

The survey also asked what kinds of information employers should be able to find out about a potential employee. Eighty-one percent of the employees believed that an employer should be able to check up on educational credentials and felony convictions, but only 57 percent thought that an employer should be able to investigate for previous medical conditions. But the majority of the workers, 70 percent, claimed that an employer should not be able to check on prior workers' compensation claims or job discrimination lawsuits. Moreover, they thought that an employer should not be able to refuse to hire someone who engages in dangerous hobbies or sports (93 percent), smokes tobacco products (93 percent), drinks alcoholic beverages (88 percent), has filed a workers' compensation claim (88 percent), has a genetic condition that predicts a major illness later in life (85 percent), has a serious disease (82 percent), is very overweight (82 percent), has been treated for a psychological or psychiatric disorder (71 percent), or is HIV positive (65 percent). The human resource executives echoed similar attitudes.[30] Considering this and several other surveys about privacy issues, two legal researchers conclude that:

> While the American public is concerned about invasions of individual privacy by government and corporations in general, employees seem to be relatively satisfied that their own employers are not abusing employees' privacy rights. Furthermore, a surprising amount of agreement exists between human resource executives and employees over what kinds of testing, screening, and monitoring procedures are appropriate for the work place.[31]

So, while it would seem that there is considerable agreement among workers and some mangers about privacy limits in the workplace, as I have shown here and in Chapter 3, many employers' actions may speak louder than their words.

BODY POLITIC(S)

While new and refined existing technologies and practices can be imposed on the body for purposes of surveillance and knowledge gathering, they can also be used to ensure docility from the recalcitrant *by taking control of the body*. In other words, if the surveillance, evidence, or threat of knowledge is not enough to render people controlled, we can always convince, cajole, or force their bodies into submission with various "treatments" or physically repressive procedures and technologies. Increasingly, these measures appear in "medicalized" forms and are offered or forced on people in the name of care for them. This phenomenon was dramatically displayed in a recent case where a "welfare mother" in Arizona had a court-ordered contraceptive device surgically implanted in her arm that would inhibit her fertility for the next five years. While there is some evidence that the Norplant device may be popular among low-income women who want to take control of *their own* fertility, it has also been suggested by some that, as a matter of public policy, welfare eligibility should be linked directly to the use of Norplant.[32] In fact, twenty such measures were introduced in thirteen states during the early 1990s. None was ultimately passed, however.

It would seem that, according to the political agenda of the New Right, some segments of the population should be stopped, by force if necessary, from having what these moral entrepreneurs consider to be "illegitimate" families. As Nancy Fraser predicted in 1989, the "coming welfare wars will be wars largely about, even against women . . . [who are] claiming benefits not as individuals but as members of 'failed' families, these recipients are effectively denied the trappings of social citizenship."[33] Of course, as I have pointed out earlier, the United States has for decades attempted to control the procreation of what were once quite openly called the "defective classes." What is so important now is that we need not go about rounding these people up in poorhouses and asylums, trying to watch and monitor their behavior as we did in the nineteenth and early twentieth centuries. The available technology makes the whole business quite simple and more politically viable, breaking down resistance (even getting the women to wait in line for the treatment) and normalizing its implementation.

Interestingly, while the government engages in profound efforts to stop the use of *illegal* "drugs," it sees fit to permit, even enforce by law, the use of *legal* "medication" regimes to control those bodies deemed out of control. In this case, "Just say no" becomes "Must say yes." The history of psychotropic "wonder drugs" is but one example. These antipsychotic medications were used in the late 1950s and 1960s in state mental hospitals to control inmates' behavior and later helped to facilitate the emptying of those hospitals in that previously institutionalized individuals were released to lead "full and productive lives in the community." The medications were used extensively, despite the fact that they often produced debilitating physical side effects such as the "Thorazine shuffle" and Parkinson's disease. In the 1990s, the Supreme Court ruled that states have the legal right to compel prison inmates to submit to antipsychotic drugs. In 1994, officials in New York State were considering a bill that would place those people being released from the state's mental hospitals—primarily the homeless and indigent—under court order to take antipsychotic and neuroleptic medications.[34]

Like the antipsychotic drugs, *electroconvulsive therapy*, or *ECT*, enjoyed a comeback of sorts in the 1980s; this psychiatric treatment creates epilepticlike seizures and convulsions as a result of an electric current being applied to the front or both sides of the brain. ECT began to be used systematically in the United States during the 1930s, and it was used extensively in state mental hospitals as a treatment for schizophrenia, despite the fact that doctors did not know why it seemed to relieve some of the symptoms. In the 1960s, however, ECT came under intense criticism as a cruel and controlling practice, and hospitals increasingly turned to the antipsychotic drugs to treat patients. But ECT reemerged in the 1980s as an increasingly common treatment for depression, especially among the elderly.[35] How have antipsychotic medications and ECT come back into favor?

In both cases, the contemporary version of these techniques have emerged in more refined and more palatable forms than their previous "modern" incarnations: a new generation of antipsychotic drugs produces few of the crippling side effects that the former drugs did, and the ECT equipment and administering procedures are free of the horrifying images dramatized in films like *One Flew Over the Cuckoo's Nest*. In fact, in the case of ECT—technically a "last-resort" treatment—private hospitals and clinics, otherwise known as "shock shops," dot the urban landscape. Both techniques, then, are being quietly normalized outside their association with the asylum, and they have become yet another disciplinary practice of everyday life. My point was well made in a *New York Times* article on the contemporary use of ECT that was entitled "With Reforms in Treatment, Shock Therapy Loses Shock." A practicing psychotherapist wrote to the newspaper a week later, stating: "Shock therapy (along with lobotomy, straight-jackets, shackles, and sterilization) is on the far right of the treatment spectrum. I believe it is symptomatic of a postmodern culture that there is a willingness on the part of some . . . to tolerate radical solutions to depression." But that is exactly my argument; in such a culture, the procedure is no longer perceived as "radical."[36]

Meanwhile, at the sound of the lunch bell at Nova Middle School in Davie, Florida, dozens of students form themselves into a line. But rather than scanning the lunch counter, these kids are waiting for their daily dose of Ritalin, a drug designed to control their "distractible," hyperactive, or impulsive behavior. Most have been diagnosed with *attention deficit disorder,* or *ADD.* "Five years ago," a journalist reports, "10 students at Nova received the medication. Now, the count is up to 40. No one knows how many more children start their day at home with a single dose, which peaks after about five hours."[37] Ritalin, despite the fact that it is a stimulant, works to help children focus on cognitive tasks, and it expands their attention span. Dr. Daniel Safer, a mental health official in Baltimore County, Maryland, estimates that 3 to 4.2 percent of American youths—from ages 5 to 18—are being treated with the stimulant. (This does not include the ones who are taking it illegally. Ritalin has reportedly become popular in the illicit drug culture, as it can produce a burst of energy, even euphoria, that lasts several hours if snorted or ingested in relatively large quantities.) Dr. Safer claims that almost twice that number of youths have ADD.

While it's clear that some children (as well as some adults) have benefited from the use of Ritalin, others contend that ADD is being vastly overdiagnosed and that Ritalin is overprescribed. Thomas Armstrong, a psychologist who wrote *The Myth of the ADD,* states:

> My criticism is that this is a model coming from a medical disease-based perspective when we should be using a model that's much more health-based. I'm not against medication for some kids under certain circumstances or in a crisis situation or in a very severe case, but I feel we rush too quickly into medications for solutions. . . . One reason for the popularity of ADD diagnosis is that it's kind of neutral. Nobody's to blame. It's not due to anything in the family, nothing to do with the classroom. Everybody is absolved of any responsibility, but the kid ends up with the label, which is a stigmatizing label. . . . We have to be very suspicious of the fact that kids are being diagnosed using very subjective or very artificial and remote kinds of approaches. . . .

Dr. Eugenio Rothe, director of the child and adolescent psychiatry outpatient clinic at Jackson Memorial Hospital in Miami, says, "There's a danger of using it as a quick fix. Rather than sit down with a kid and find out what's bothering him, some may give a pill and that's it." He argues that some pediatricians may be writing prescriptions based primarily on parents' and teachers' complaints. "I'm sure there are kids medicated inappropriately for behavioral control and not true ADD," he says.[38]

In a very different mode of controlling behavior, defense contractors and research labs are turning their post–Cold War attention to the burgeoning "high-tech" security market in order to develop what are referred to as "less-than-lethal weapons" for police use. If successful, the police say, an arsenal of nonlethal weapons could save lives and spare them the cost of all those pesky excessive-force lawsuits. Los Angeles police and others have, in the past, deployed Mace and "pepper" sprays and the infamous baton "choke hold." But now, new devices are making headway. Various forms of "stun guns" are being deployed, including one prototype that shoots a stream of coffee-colored "sticky goo" that entangles an unruly arrestee. At Lawrence Livermore Labs in California, researchers are experimenting with high-intensity strobe lights that incapacitate people, low-frequency sounds that disorient and create nausea, and rapidly expanding foam that can fill a cell, for example, and block the sight and hearing of rioting prisoners. A similar device may be installed in the rear seat of police cars to subdue a violent passenger.

As states like California struggle to deal with exploding prison populations, officials are searching for ways to cut costs, like reducing staff. For example, at the two-year-old Calipatria Facility, just north of the Mexican boarder, authorities have installed an electrified fence that carries 4,000 volts and 650 milliamperes of power. About 70 milliamperes is enough to kill a human being. For anyone trying to escape, this amounts to an automatic death sentence. The warden of the facility states that unlike a guard, "the fence doesn't get distracted, it doesn't look away for a moment and it doesn't get tired." He has no problem using the fence, since the prison already has a "lethal perimeter" within which guards are instructed to "shoot to kill" an escapee. More than twenty additional California prisons are expected to get the fences in the next few years.[39] Another fascinating device currently in use in about 150 locations in the country is an electronic "stun belt" that is strapped around a defendant's waist at trial or may be used on prisoners, etc. The REACT belt, manufactured by Stun-tech, Inc., of Cleveland, is a 4-inch-wide elastic band that is powered by a battery at the kidney and has a remote control. When activated, the device sends a shock of 50,000 volts in eight-second bursts to the person's back muscles—enough to "make subjects scream and drop to the floor, writhing in pain." The company says that the feeling can be summed up in one word: "devastation."[40]

Finally, the ultimate "devastation" comes in the form of a death sentence. In the 1990s, state after state brought back executions as a supposed deterrence to criminal behavior (despite the fact that there is simply no evidence that capital punishment functions in this way). Yet it is clear that the revival of the death sentence is about public vengeance that, statistically, is more likely to be directed against African-Americans than against whites who commit the same crimes. While state-sponsored executions are obviously not part of everyday of life and have, fundamentally, little to do with my notion of meticulous rituals, there are certain similarities. Unlike the public display of brutality and reprisal that the scaffold provided, today's executions are sanitized, medical procedures that culminate in a bureaucratic death. In this way, they reflect— much like drug testing, the p-graph, Norplant, ECT, and the other techniques I have described—a surrender of the fundamental problem of social control to science and technology. A state execution, once medicalized, is no longer a "horrible" event; it becomes simply another pill swallowed, a test taken, or a medical procedure submitted to. Here is how one journalist described the execution of a man in Texas in 1994:

> Under brilliant fluorescent lights, Steven Ray Netherie, a 33-year-old Tennessean, convicted of killing a Dallas policeman, lies splayed on a gurney. The sight is stunning and confusing, not quite hospital, not quite death chamber. Gurney is a medical word for a cot or a stretcher on wheels. But this is a stainless steel platform, bolted permanently to the floor. The medical illusion is further enhanced by the IV tubes running into each arm. One serves as a back up. But the nine thick leather restraints convey the reality. Netherie stares at the ceiling. He swallows, he wets his mouth. The warden calls for the last words. Netherie closes his eyes and recites a prayer in a halting drawl. Within seconds, the executioner, hidden behind a one-way mirror, starts to push eight syringes sequentially. In short order, they will induce unconsciousness, paralyze the diaphragm to stop breathing and cause cardiac arrest.

The chemicals in the IV are actually referred to as "medicine" by the prison director. After the inmate is killed and pronounced dead, a prison spokesman issues this statement in a dispassionate, almost mechanical voice:

> The execution of Steven Ray Netherie was carried out. He was taken from the holding cell at 12:06, strapped to a gurney at 12:07, was given an opportunity to make a last statement at 12:21, in which he said, "Well, I just wanted to ask people to pray for two families, my fami-

ly and the family of Officer McCarthy. I appreciate their
prayers, Lord Jesus, receive my spirit. Amen." The lethal
chemicals were introduced at 12:22, completed at 12:24
and Steven Ray Netherie was pronounced dead at 12:30.

The bureaucratic administration of death is complete: File deleted.[41]

By medicalizing executions with lethal injection, the state of Texas,
like twenty-four other states that have adopted the procedure, is attempting to "humanize" an inherently inhuman activity. "Lethal injection is
usually brief, efficient and antiseptic," said the journalist who witnessed
this killing. As a former attorney general for the state observed, "It's not
a lot different from putting a dog to sleep." Criminologist James
Marcourt states: "Electrocutions were violent. But electrocutions were
less violent than public hanging. Now, we have lethal injection, which is
obviously less violent than electrocution, so we're seeing this nice pro-
gression along a continuum of technology. Like I said, it's basically an
anti-climatic event. It's much more palatable to the public." And the chief
of the Texas Prison System is quoted as saying, "We don't want to make
a spectacle out of it, or give it the flavor of a circus or a carnival."[42] But
apparently one TV talk-show host wanted to do just that; he is suing the
State of California in an attempt to get an execution televised. I suspect,
however, that the ratings for such a show would be a disappointment.
Surely the public would prefer the exciting, fast-paced images of medical
technology, trauma, and death that are dramatized on the latest prime-
time hospital show.

How do we experience a situation where our bodies are becoming a
central target of knowledge and social control? It is said that the postmodern self personifies the multiple contradictions of the postmodern
condition and may result in "intense emotional experiences shaped by
anxiety, alienation, resentment, and detachment from others."[43] It seems
to me that technologies or practices that permit our bodies to "speak the
truth," whether we want that voice to be heard or not, or, alternatively,
that control and restrict our bodies from being what they are, generate
these very emotional states as they "detach" us from ourselves. Like the
person whose capable mind is trapped in a degenerative frame, we are
betrayed and abandoned by the physical expression of who we are.
Hanson poetically describes this apparent double-cross in the case of the
lie detector:

> The two machines commune together as the polygraph
> reaches out to embrace the subject's body with bands,
> tubes, and clips. The body responds lover-like to the
> touch, whispering secrets to the polygraph in tiny
> squeezes, twinges, thrills, and nudges. Both the machines

are treacherous. The body, seduced by the polygraph's embrace, thoughtlessly prattles the confidences it shares with the subject's mind. The polygraph, a false and uncaring confidant, publishes the secrets it has learned on a chart to read. The subject as mind, powerless to chaperon the affair, watches helplessly as the carnal entwine of the machines produces its undoing.[44]

What are our options to resist this courtship? One is, of course, self-control, to behave, to stay "clean," to "Just say no." The other strategy is to try to trick our bodies into not giving us away—a process that is sure to reinforce the personal troubles of the postmodern self and, if successful, to send the technicians scurrying to perfect a more "reliable instrument."

NOTES

1. American Management Association (AMA), *AMA Survey on Workplace Drug Testing and Drug Abuse Policies*. New York: American Management Association, 1994.
2. "At Work, a Different Test for Drugs." *New York Times,* January 21, 1996: F11.
3. *Abuscreen Ontrack* by Roche Diagnostic Systems, 1989.
4. Steven L. Nock, *The Costs of Privacy: Surveillance and Reputation in America.* New York: De Gruyter, 1989.
5. Ibid., 102.
6. F. Allan Hanson, *Testing Testing: Social Consequences of the Examined Life.* Berkeley: University of California Press, 1993: 128.
7. Ibid.
8. "At Work, a Different Test for Drugs." *New York Times,* January 21, 1996: F11.
9. "Workers Gain Privacy Rights by Legislation, Judicial Action." *National Law Journal,* April 9, 1990.
10. "Justices to Take Up Case of Schools' Drug Testing." *New York Times,* March 29, 1995: A12.
11. Hanson, 1993: 68.
12. U.S. Congress, Office of Technology Assessment, 1983 (cited in Nock 1993: 89–90).
13. Nock, 1993: 90–91.
14. Michel Foucault, *Discipline and Punish: The Birth of the Prison.* Trans. A. M. Sheridan. New York: Pantheon, 1979: 193.
15. "Debatable Device: Privacy, Technology Collide in a Dispute over Intimate Test." *Wall Street Journal,* February 3, 1993: 1.

16. "The Indelicate Art of Telling Adults How to Have Sex." *New York Times*, May 16, 1993: E18.
17. Ibid.
18. Dorothy Nelkin and Lawrence Tancredi, *Dangerous Diagnostics: The Social Power of Biological Information*. Chicago: University of Chicago Press, [1989] 1994: 160–61.
19. "Faster, More Accurate Fingerprint Matching." *New York Times*, October 11, 1992: F9.
20. "Fingerprint System Extends Arm of the Law." *New York Times*, November 12, 1993: B11.
21. "Fingerprinting Targets Welfare Fraud." *Lawrence Journal-World*, January 23, 1994: A9.
22. "The Hand's Shape: Unique and Useful for Identity Check." *New York Times*, October 21, 1992: C5.
23. "Minn. Debates Bill to Prohibit Genetic Testing." *National Underwriter, Property & Casualty/Risk & Benefits Management Edition*. March 20, 1995: 24.
24. "Rebuilding Confidence in Confidentiality." *National Underwriter, Life & Health/Financial Services Edition*. October 23, 1995: 35.
25. Nelkin and Tancredi, 1994: ix–x.
26. "Business Using Therapy Data to Lower Costs." *New York Times*, April 12, 1994: A1.
27. "Employee Beware: The Boss May Be Listening." *Wall Street Journal*, July 29, 1994: C1.
28. "Medical Data Gathered by Firms Can Prove Less Than Confidential." *Wall Street Journal*, May 19, 1994: A1.
29. Ibid.
30. Lewis Harris and Associates, *Work Place Health and Privacy Issues: A Survey of Private Sector Employees and Leaders*. New York, 1994.
31. "Public Expresses Privacy Concerns." *Law & Policy Reporter*, December 1994: 206.
32. "Where the Norplant Debate Hits Home." *New York Times*, March 7, 1993: 17.
33. Nancy Fraser, *Unruly Practices: Power, Discourse, and Gender in Contemporary Social Theory*. Minneapolis: University of Minnesota Press, 1989: 144, 152–53.
34. Peter Breggin, "Let's Not 'Treat' the Problem of Homelessness with Drugs." *New York Times*, June 26, 1994: E6.
35. Carol A. B. Warren and Kathleen A. K. Levy, "Electroconvulsive Therapy and the Elderly." *Journal of Aging Studies* 5, 1991: 309–27.
36. "With Reforms in Treatment, Shock Therapy Loses Shock." *New York Times*, July 19, 1993: A1; and "Shock Therapy Still Causes Brain Damage." *New York Times*, August 1, 1993: E14.

37. "As More Children Use Ritalin, Debate over Drug Grows." *Dallas Morning News*, December 29, 1995: 15C.

38. "A Wonder Drug's Worst Side Effect; Kids Turning to Easy-to-Get Ritalin for a Quick—and Sometimes Deadly—High." *Washington Post*, February 5, 1996: A1; "SchoolWatch; Psychologist: ADD Is Abused Diagnosis." *Atlanta Journal and Constitution*, January 16, 1996: B3; and "Reading, Writing and Ritalin." *New York Times*, October 21, 1995: A21.

39. "New Fence Could Kill Escapees." *Kansas City Star*, November 20, 1993: A9.

40. "Order in the Court—with Shocking Restraint." *Lawrence Journal-World*, April 9, 1994: 10D.

41. John Burnett, "Capital Punishment—Part Two." *National Public Radio—All Things Considered*, September 27, 1994.

42. Ibid.

43. Norman K. Denzin, *Images of Postmodern Society: Social Theory and Contemporary Cinema*. Newbury Park, Calif.: Sage, 1991: vii.

44. Hanson, 1993: 93.

5

The Revolution
Will Not Be Televised

Thousands of eyes posited everywhere, mobile attentions ever at the alert, a long hierarchized network.
—Michel Foucault

What I apprehend immediately when I hear the branches cracking behind me is not that there is someone there; it is that I am vulnerable; that I have a body which can be hurt; that I occupy a place and I cannot in any case escape from this space in which I am without defense—in short, I am seen.[1]
—Jean-Paul Sartre

In the future, everyone will be famous for fifteen minutes.
—Andy Warhol

The purpose of this book has been to offer an account of some of the disciplinary practices that have become part of postmodern life. Following the work of Michel Foucault, I have centered my observations on the practices that intersect power, knowledge, and the body. Most generally, I have included "micro" techniques of discipline—often enhanced by the use of new information, visual, communication, and medical technologies—that target and treat the body as an object to be watched, assessed, and manipulated. These local, "meticulous rituals of power" are the knowledge-gathering activities that involve surveillance, information, and evidence collection and analysis that increasingly compose our daily lives as workers, consumers, and community members. I have argued that these new disciplinary techniques must be understood as a product both of important, long-term processes set in motion with the onset of modernity and of the emerging cultural context of postmodernity. One of my goals has been to show how we appear to be building a "community *of* corrections" where there has been a tendency to normalize the presence of formal social control in everyday life. Much like the reformers of nineteenth century, contemporary advocates of "community-based" punishment and social control seek to make justice more effective and more efficient. Yet, as I have shown, as they have decentralized the justice system, its techniques and procedures have been broken down and adapted for use in schools, workplaces, and other community institutions. "But perhaps the most important effect of the carceral system and its extension well beyond legal imprisonment is," according to Foucault, "that it succeeds in making the power to punish natural and legitimate, in lowering at least the threshold of tolerance to penalty."[2]

But how did all this happen? "There was no revolution," one journalist declares, "no totalitarian takeover, no war bringing the collapse of world-wide democracy. But by an invention here and a new computer application there, American culture is nearing the point forwarded by those who feared technology could breed a new kind of oppression."[3] Yet, while many of us are subjected to this new despotism, few, it would seem, see or appreciate the implications of this "quiet" revolution. One reason, as I have tried to show, is that these disciplinary practices often work in the background; we may not even know they exist, and even if we do, they rarely, in and of themselves, give cause for serious concern. Take, for example, the "tagging" of merchandise in stores to prevent shoplifting. If we were confronted as we left a business and were "patted down" physically, people would be outraged. Yet, since the technology permits us to be "electronically" frisked, we generally consent to this surveillance ceremony. But at the same time, the ritualistic removing of the tags at the checkout line and the presence of the barrierlike scanners at the doors remind us that we are in fact being watched. How many of us still cringe when we exit, knowing that we have done nothing wrong, but still slightly afraid of the alarms, fearful that an absentminded clerk might have forgotten to remove a tag. Even the more confrontive disciplinary rituals such as random drug screens are quickly routinized into common, everyday practices that soon lose their sense of transgression. "Who cares if someone tapes my conversation at the local donut shop?" someone will declare; "What difference does it make if some big company knows all about me?" another asks. "People should be tested for drugs," most seem to say; "They can test me, I have nothing to hide." Fragmented and piecemeal, quiet and habitual—and often convincingly productive—meticulous rituals elicit only minor resistance.

Yet these new habits, no matter how small or seemingly trivial, have their own significance, for they define a certain mode of political investment in the body. That is, they are the concrete manifestation of the ways in which our bodily lives are shaped, manipulated, and controlled by public and private organizations and by the people who have authority over us. These are the politics of social control in the workplace, the school, the home, and the community. But since they often appear as a "nudge" here and a "twist" there, few of us experience them as anything like "oppression." But taken together, these "small acts of cunning," as Foucault called them, constitute the building blocks of what I would argue is a rapidly emerging culture of surveillance—a society of "judges," exercising the "power to punish" everywhere, a society increasingly lacking in personal privacy and individual trust and a viable public life that supports and maintains democratic values and practices.

I do not claim that the disciplinary practices I have identified are put in place with impunity, that they are universally accepted, or even that they work in accordance with their proponents' claims. Development is uneven; some resistance is always present. There is competition among providers of new technology, some of it designed to thwart the efforts of others. While the phone companies sell us CallerID and CallTrace, for example, they also market CallBlocker to prevent these other functions. People do fake drug tests, employers make exceptions, and probations officers "work" with violators trying to avoid revocations. Like the invention of the asylum itself, the new techniques are often touted as embodying all the ideal virtues of justice, while being more effective, less expensive, and more "civilized" than what came before. The prison, for example, was more "humane" than the scaffold; now that the reality of the penitentiary can no longer be concealed (or its cost tolerated), the electronic anklet bracelet is "kinder and gentler" and more practical than the institution. Each failure, it seems, only serves to justify and bring about a new generation of disciplinary mechanisms.

FORGET "BIG BROTHER"

When I speak about the emergence of this "culture of surveillance," someone invariably asks, "Who is doing all this? Who's behind it? Who is 'Big Brother'?" "There is no 'Big Brother,'" I tell them; *we* are him. Rather than appear simply "from the top down" or originate from a small group of identifiable individuals or even a particular organization, disciplinary power, I argue, is advanced, directly or indirectly, by all of us. It is not orchestrated by only a few or part of some master plan that is simply imposed on us; rather, disciplinary power is "bidirectional," flowing from top to bottom and vice versa. So while Ronald Reagan can issue an executive order that demands that all federal workers be tested for drugs, an ex-auto mechanic can start marketing and selling video cameras to school districts for their buses. While the FBI can help push a wiretap bill through Congress, an employer in your hometown may initiate "integrity" testing of all job applicants. A government agency or giant corporation may set out to create a new surveillance gadget, but it seems just as likely that a university professor will develop one—or, importantly, the basis for a *potential* one—for no other reason than "curiosity" or to get a promotion. A young computer software designer may develop a new program because its capabilities are "cool," rather than seeing it as an employee-monitoring tool. A grade school teacher may get a grant to adopt bar-code scanning in the classroom simply because the technology is there and because to use it "sounds like a good idea."

This is *not* to suggest that the culture of surveillance emerges "by accident." Some people have a vested interest in creating, selling, and implementing "meticulous rituals," and others may be in a position to exercise this kind of control and benefit from it in different ways. Yet even they are, ultimately, not exempt from the gaze of that "long hierarchized network" Foucault refers to. In this way, as I have argued, we are all involved and enmeshed within a grid of power relations that are highly intentional and purposeful, arrangements that can be more or less hierarchical and unequal but are never simply one-directional. So while a police officer can surveil suspects with a new high-tech scanner, the department can "keep an eye" on the officer by installing a videocam in the patrol car. Similarly, a teacher can make "normalizing judgments" about students using a computer program, only to find that school administrators can use the same program to assess the teacher's "performance" in the classroom.

Today's culture of surveillance, I would argue, is being built on a foundation of seduction, desire, fear, and salvation. We all advance disciplinary power when we go about naïvely—and with blind faith and arrogance—trying to "make things better," uncritically accepting the arguments of those that claim to be doing so and always assuming that, in fact, we can. This applies to anyone, across the political spectrum. "The road to hell," the saying goes, "is paved with good intentions." While some of the effects I have described in this book may be the "unintended consequences" of such good intentions, they are consequences nonetheless, and, it seems, they are rarely considered in the discussion. We extend the bounds of the culture of surveillance when we turn our backs on the important relationship between knowledge and power, when we take science—physical, medical, and social—at its word or assume that all technological change is always "for the better." There are often very compelling reasons why it seems that decisions are made to test people for drugs, to fingerprint welfare recipients, or to put surveillance cameras on school buses. After all, we need to "deal with the problem" (even if we have little idea of just what the problem actually is) or, better yet, because "something might happen." Why not take steps to prevent it? We are easily seduced by the image of a protected, peaceful order. We are a people who like things to "work," to be efficient, to be predictable, to "make sense." We are persuaded and charmed by politicians promising social stability, school administrators ensuring well-behaved children, and developers offering us the "serene fortress" of the gated community. We desire to eliminate risk, but at what price? Listen to those who become crusaders after a tragedy strikes their lives: the phenomenon (whatever it is—drug addiction, drunk driving, child molestation— it doesn't matter) will be stopped "at all cost," "to prevent this tragedy from happening to someone else"; "if one life can be saved, it will be worth it." Will it? Obviously, we want to stop needless loss of life and injury, but on what basis and with what values do we evaluate the choice between reducing life's risks and tragedies by some unknown amount versus limiting our constitutional rights and personal freedoms? Put another way, is it worth surviving the risks of life only to end up "living" in a surveillance society?

We support, actively or passively, the creation of disciplinary practices, irrationally believing that they will be deployed exclusively "on those other folks," only to find that we have become the next target. So we construct the culture of surveillance as well when we consume products that either make us the potential targets of surveillance or, alternatively, give us the tools to watch others. Here, the everyday act of consumption—so central to the organization of late capitalism—becomes directly tied to the distribution and spread of disciplinary technology. If the company hasn't already done so, we are quite willing to "wire" ourselves in with "cell" phones, pagers, and email, and we rush to buy the latest products that offer us access to the "Net" and the "Web" (the irony of this new language should not be ignored). We also bring home the machines to monitor our kids' phone calls, to keep an eye on their driving, or even to test them for drugs. We buy the videocams and use them to document our own movements, or we turn them on our friends, neighbors, or strangers. *America's Funniest Home Videos* receives more than two thousand clips a day. According to the host, "everybody gets their Andy Warhol fifteen minutes. It's like driving by and looking into people's windows"[4] News networks will pay handsomely for amateur tapes of "important" events that they can then broadcast over and over again. In a culture of voyeurs, there is always plenty of footage. Interestingly, as the case of the Rodney King beating illustrates, we can even use these devices to "turn the tables" on those who abuse their position. Some argue that this signals the "democratization of surveillance," offering ordinary citizens the power to challenge authorities. Yet, this strikes me as a contradiction in terms. A democratic society ensures and protects everyone's personal privacy; it does not facilitate universal *visibility*.

The imperative of more and more social control is also a function of fear. Steven Nock claims that increased formal surveillance results from our need to establish "reputations" and trust because, in a society of strangers, "How can we trust the people we see but do not know; those who live near us, who work near us, who must sometimes be counted on to help us?"[5] Yet, I would argue that, in our contemporary culture, it would seem that the "stranger" is more than someone without a reputation; what we really fear is the stranger assumed to exist *within us all*. In the culture of hysteria, everyone is a potential suspect; otherwise, why would people who have established, "good" reputations still be subjected to surveillance ceremonies? Nock cites the example of the "highly respected civic leader" who is trusted; "His word is believed; his promise accepted." Yet, at the height of the "war on drugs," a proposal was made in my hometown that five city commissioners present themselves for drug screening in order to make a public statement that the town was "drug-free." The commissioners voted against the proposal, 3 to 2, and the editor of the local newspaper proceeded to question the motives of those who had voted against it. The message is clear: If you refuse to consent to disciplinary rituals, you must have something to hide.

It seems that we indeed trust no one. As I have argued, our primary sources of cultural knowledge, the popular media and cinema, have turned everyday life into a theatrical drama where the most compelling stories are those that recount lives filled with uncertainty, unpredictability, and tragedy. "Watch out! You could be next!" the media scream out. We therefore become convinced that our only recourse against the apparent tide of problems we face is to "keep on eye on" everyone. We are therefore seduced into believing that even our own subjection is an unfortunate but necessary condition. Is fear an irrational response then? No. Not only are the media accounts powerfully convincing, but our fears *are* grounded in a reality. The United States is a relatively dangerous place; I am not suggesting that crime, youth violence, drugs, and other social ills are not "real." What I am saying is that we need to be aware of the role played by the media in shaping the process of how we come to "know" and believe we understand the nature of those problems.

This cultural hysteria—generated by docudramas, prime-time sensational journalism, and made-for-TV movies "based on the true story"—creates a fertile market for those selling "science" and the technological "fixes" they claim will bring knowledge and certainty to ease our fears. Political problems become technical ones when we are gripped by fear and we long for the salvation of easy "solutions." But what have we bargained for when we surrender the fundamental problem of social control to science and technology? Ironically, while the videocam is used to "create" this hysteria through television and the cinema, it is offered as our salvation as well. "Just put up a camera" they say, and the problems will go away. In the case of the school bus, for example, once the camera is in place, no one has to bother teaching children *why* they should behave, it's enough just to get them to do it. This begs the question, How will they act when they are not under the gaze of the camera? Of course, the logical outcome of this "solution" is to make sure that they are *always* under its watchful eye.

How do we maintain anything deserving to be called a democratic society in the face of all this? I am not referring simply to the act of voting (although that is at issue also), as much as I am to the notion of democracy as an ongoing, daily accomplishment that is practiced and maintained both in human relationships and by mediating institutions. *Democracy* in this sense means not only ensuring our constitutionally given rights but also fostering what we might call the characteristics of a "good society"[6]—a society where citizens are able to maintain a degree of trust in the individuals and organizations that they encounter; a society that is "civil" in every sense of the word; a society that ensures human rights and dignities and respects individual difference. For years, social and political scholars have asserted that a fundamental characteristic of such a society is a viable public life—one that includes both public space (e.g., streets, parks, community markets, meeting places, schools, and the like) and a civic discourse (i.e., something like "public opinion"). If Enlightenment reason and democratic ideals offer us any hope, it is in the notion that people can come together and rationally decide what is in their best interest and for the common good.

But in today's culture, how is this possible? As more and more of this "public" space is brought under the gaze of surveillance, and as meticulous rituals permeate our daily lives, "there is nowhere to hide," as Gary Marx puts it. "A citizen's ability to evade this surveillance is diminishing. To venture into a shopping mall, bank, subway, sometimes even a bathroom is to perform before an unknown audience."[7] Even if this kind of surveillance is relatively "seamless" as I have argued, it may function to undermine our willingness to participate in civic life and "to speak our minds as clearly, openly, and imaginatively as we can."[8] Driven out of the public sphere, we retreat to the "private life" of home only to find that, increasingly, it is not private at all. Here, public opinion has been replaced by the mass-mediated "storytelling" of high-profile media stars who "inform" us about what to buy, how to vote, and what is and what is not a "social problem." Our homes will be increasingly "hardwired" with new telecommunication links that offer corporations unprecedented access to our habits, buying preferences, and financial status.[9] Meanwhile, some of the same technologies can be used to convert some people's homes into "virtual" prisons as they are remotely monitored under the watchful eye of authorities or, in other instances, as the devices enable suspicious parents to listen in on their teenagers' phone calls, to videotape the baby-sitter, or to riffle through each other's email. With the contemporary blurring of boundaries between notions of "public" and "private," between "real" freedom and its simulation, it is easy to see how "democracy" could become little more than a media illusion on the postmodern landscape.

BACK FROM THE ABYSS

All this sounds pretty bleak, doesn't it? Now that we have arrived at the crumbling edge of the cliff, it's time to turn to me and say, "OK, now what? You brought us here; what do we do about it?" This is the point in which many so-called cultural critics end their book by offering some vague and hopeful agenda for the future, evoking some ideal society that will somehow mysteriously spring forth from the rubble. Well, I have no such agenda to offer. To do so would contradict much of what I have written here. Some readers may respond to this by saying, "See, it's easy to be critical and much harder to come up with solutions." But I don't agree; both criticism and solutions are extremely difficult. The first step, I would argue, is understanding; to learn that there is, indeed, a crumbling ledge out there to be cautious of; to see it through the haze of confusion, accepted wisdom, and just plain foolishness.

Since advocating leaping into the abyss would effectively end our discussion here, let's assume we choose to confront the surveillance society. Let's further assume that, while possible, a radically different culture is not likely to emerge anytime soon. After all, as I have tried to show, much of what we live with today is grounded in a legacy of Western thought and practice dating back several centuries. It is also firmly lodged in the basic day-to-day functioning of the society. Given these assumptions, what can we do, as individuals, to counter disciplinary practices? One strategy is to simply drop out of the culture entirely. This is the tactic of many who have retreated to places like Idaho and other western states, part of the so-called radical survivalist movement. Interestingly, these "counterculture" groups characterize themselves as living "off the grid" of credit cards, television, public utilities, and the consumer society. While these folks appear to be alert to some of the issues I have raised, their racism and rampantly conspiratorial "Big Brother" paranoia about the government misses the mark completely and makes them quite an unattractive lot to sign on with.

An alternative position, however, is one of active resistance. If we accept the premise that much of the exercise of this kind of power takes place in the form of "local" micropractices that are present in our every-day lives, then the sites of opposition are right before us. They are in our own homes, workplaces, schools, and communities. We don't need to form a counterinsurgency movement to storm Washington, D.C. In fact, such an exercise, while possibly symbolic, would not likely amount to much. Rather, when some school board members in your community assert that student athletes should be tested for drugs, demand that they demonstrate that drug abuse is indeed a problem. Next time you telephone a business and a recording tells you that your call is being monitored "for your protection," ask to speak to a supervisor, and tell that person that you disapprove of the practice. When your state legislature debates the merits of fingerprinting drivers'-license applicants (and they will, likely, soon), call your representative's office and ask her or him to vote against it. The next time someone carries on about the wonders of the latest digital gadget, acknowledge its potential benefits but remind the speaker that there may be a down side to the product's use. Talk with your kids, openly and honestly, about both the allure and the dangers of drug use. In fact, turn off the television, log off the computer, unclip the beeper, and take your kid for a walk around the block. Wave to your neighbors. Well, you get the point. . . .

NOTES

1. Jean-Paul Sartre, "The Other and His Look," in Justin Treller, ed., *To Freedom Condemned.* New York: Philosophical Library, 1960: 37.
2. Michel Foucault, *Discipline and Punish: The Birth of the Prison.* Trans. A. M. Sheridan. New York: Pantheon, 1979: 301.
3. "Surveillance Extends Everywhere." *Lincoln Star,* May 19, 1994: 7.
4. Quoted in Lili Berko, "Surveying the Surveilled: Video, Space, and Subjectivity." *Quarterly Review of Film and Video* 14, 1992: 61–91.
5. Steven L. Nock, *The Costs of Privacy: Surveillance and Reputation in America.* New York: De Gruyter, 1989: 3.
6. Robert N. Bellah, Richard Madsen, William M. Sullivan, Ann Swindler, and Steven M. Tipton, *The Good Society.* New York: Knopf, 1991.
7. Gary T. Marx, quoted in Berko, 1992: 86.
8. Jeffrey C. Goldfarb, *The Cynical Society.* Chicago: University of Chicago Press, 1991: 182.
9. So-called futurists tell us that these new communication technologies will make us citizens in a new "global village," but life in these "virtual," simulated communities may offer us little knowledge about how to actually survive in our own

Selected References

Altheide, David, "Electronic Media and State Control: The Case of Azscam." *Sociological Quarterly* 34, 1993: 53–69.

———, "Gonzo Justice." *Symbolic Interaction* 15, 1993: 69–86.

———, *Media Power*. Newbury Park, Calif.: Sage, 1985.

American Management Association (AMA), *AMA Survey on Workplace Drug Testing and Drug Abuse Policies*. New York: American Management Association, 1994.

Baudrillard, Jean, *Simulations*. New York: Semiotext(e), 1983.

Bellah, Robert N., Richard Madsen, William M. Sullivan, Ann Swindler, and Steven M. Tipton, *The Good Society*. New York: Knopf, 1991.

Bentham, Jeremy, "Preface." In Miran Bozovic, ed., *The Panopticon Writings*. London: Verso, 1995: 32.

Berko, Lili, "Surveying the Surveilled: Video, Space, and Subjectivity." *Quarterly Review of Film and Video* 14, 1992: 61–91.

Best, Steven, "Foucault, Postmodernism, and Social Theory." In David R. Dickens and Andrea Fontana, eds., *Postmodernism and Social Inquiry*. New York: Guilford, 1994.

Conrad, Peter, and Joseph Schneider, *Deviance and Medicalization: From Badness to Sickness*. St. Louis: Mosby, 1980; and Malcolm Spector, "Beyond Crime: Seven Methods to Control Troublesome Rascals." In H. L. Ross, ed., *Law and Deviance*. Beverly Hills: Sage, 1981:127–58.

Corbett, Ronald, and Gary T. Marx, "Critique: No Soul in the New Machine: Technofallacies in the Electronic Monitoring Movement." *Justice Quarterly* 8, September, 1991: 403.

Davis, Mike, *City of Quartz: Excavating the Future in Los Angeles*. London: Verso, 1990.

Denzin, Norman K., *Images of Postmodern Society: Social Theory and Contemporary Cinema*. London: Sage, 1991.

Dumm, Thomas, *Democracy and Punishment: Disciplinary Origins of the United States*. Madison: University of Wisconsin Press, 1987.

Emerson, Robert M., and Sheldon M. Messinger, "The Micro-Politics of Trouble." *Social Problems* 25, 1977 :121–34.

Foucault, Michel, *Discipline and Punish: The Birth of the Prison*. Trans. A. M. Sheridan. New York: Pantheon, 1977.

———, "Afterword: The Subject of Power." In Hubert L. Dreyfus and Paul Rabinow, eds., *Michel Foucault: Beyond Structuralism and Hermeneutics*. Berkeley: University of California Press, 1983.

Fraser, Nancy, *Unruly Practices: Power, Discourse, and Gender in Contemporary Social Theory*. Minneapolis: University of Minnesota Press, 1989.

Friedman, Lawrence, *A History of American Law*. New York: Simon and Schuster, 1973.

Gandy, Oscar, Jr., *The Panoptic Sort: A Political Economy of Personal Information.* Boulder, Colo.: Westview, 1993: 2.

Goldfarb, Jeffrey C., *The Cynical Society.* Chicago: University of Chicago Press, 1991.

Hanson, F. Allan, *Testing Testing: Social Consequences of the Examined Life.* Berkeley: University of California Press, 1993.

Harris, Lewis, and Associates, *Work Place Health and Privacy Issues: A Survey of Private Sector Employees and Leaders.* New York: 1994.

Hodges, V. G., and B. Blythe, "Improving Service Delivery to High-Risk Families: Home-Based Practice." *Journal of Families in Society: The Journal of Contemporary HumanServices* 73, 1992.

Holman, John E., and James F. Quinn, "Dysphoria and Electronically Monitored Home Confinement." *Deviant Behavior* 13, 1992: 21–32.

Humphreys, Keith, and Julian Rappaport, "From the Community Mental Health Movement to the War on Drugs: A Study in the Definitions of Social Problems." *American Psychologist* 48, 1993: 896.

Krier, Dan, and Willliam G. Staples, "Seen but Unseen: Part-time Faculty and Institutional Surveillance and Control." *American Sociologist* 24, 1994: 119–34.

Lewis, Orlando, *The Development of American Prisons and Prison Customs, 1776–1845.* Albany: Prison Association of New York, [1922] 1967.

Lewis, W. David, *From Newgate to Dannemora.* Ithaca, N.Y.: Cornell University Press, 1975.

Lowe, Donald, *The Body in Late Capitalism USA.* Durham, N.C.: Duke University Press, 1995.

Lyon, David, "The New Surveillance: Electronic Technologies and the Maximum Security Society." *Crime, Law and Social Change* 18, 1992: 159–75.

Morse Earle, Alice, *Curious Punishments of Bygone Days.* Rutland, Vt.: Charles E. Tenant, 1972.

Nelkin, Dorothy, and Lawrence Tancredi, *Dangerous Diagnostics: The Social Power of Biological Information.* Chicago: University of Chicago Press, [1989] 1994.

Nock, Steven L., *The Costs of Privacy: Surveillance and Reputation in America.* New York: De Gruyter, 1989.

Petersilia, Joan, *Expanding Options for Criminal Sentencing.* Santa Monica, Calif.: RAND, 1987.

Rothman, David, *Conscience and Convenience: The Asylum and Its Alternatives in Progressive America.* Boston: Little, Brown, 1980.

———, *The Discovery of the Asylum: Social Order and Disorder in the New Republic.* Boston: Little, Brown, 1971.

Smith, H. Jeff, *Managing Privacy: Information, Technology, and Corporate America.* Chapel Hill: University of North Carolina Press, 1994.

Staples, William G., *Castles of Our Conscience: Social Control and the American State, 1800–1985.* New Brunswick, N.J.: Rutgers University Press, 1991.

———, "Small Acts of Cunning: Disciplinary Practices in Contemporary Life." *Sociological Quarterly* 35, 1994: 645–64.

Warren, Carol A. B., and Kathleen A. K. Levy, "Electroconvulsive Therapy and the Elderly." *Journal of Aging Studies* 5, 1991: 309–27.

Woods, L. J., "HomeBased Family Therapy." *Social Work* 33, 1988: 211–14.

Index